Praise the Lord
and
Pass the Chemo

A Hopeful Response to
a Hard Reality

Elaine W. Miller

ENDORSEMENTS

"A contagious joy infects the pages of *Praise the Lord and Pass the Chemo*. Elaine W. Miller refuses to let a leukemia diagnosis steal her joy. Trusting God and believing he fights for her, she knows her eternity in heaven is secure. That puts her in a win-win position — surrendered to whatever God pleases to do. Her faith-filled perspective facing a potential death sentence offers encouragement and hope to others walking through dark, uncertain places. They will learn to laugh at cancer and find unexpected blessings in the journey. This sweet book by my precious friend is a shout-out to the Lord she loves with all her heart."

Dianne Barker, Speaker, radio host, and author,
I Don't Chase the Garbage Truck Down the Street in My Bathrobe Anymore! Organizing for the Maximum Life

Cancer does a lot of things, but it doesn't change who God is or His plans and purposes for our lives. Elaine Miller understands that, and she chose to trust God and glorify Him while facing her diagnosis. In *Praise the Lord and Pass the Chemo*, she acknowledges that cancer isn't fun, but she also shows us that with the right perspective we can walk through it victoriously. Thank you, Elaine, for gifting your readers with these important truths.

Twila Belk — cancer survivor, speaker, and author
of seven books, including *The Power to Be: Be Still,
Be Grateful, Be Strong, Be Courageous*

"Elaine W. Miller has given a precious gift to those facing the challenge of cancer or who are walking the road together with them. This new book is a remarkable treasure trove of wisdom gained from God's word in the fires of personal experience. There is depth, hope, understanding, and victory in Jesus here. My highest recommendation."

David Bruce Linn, Alliance Northeastern
District Superintendent C&MA

As a personal friend of Elaine's it has been a joy to read this book. In one sense it is a step of obedience, in another, a testimony to the healing power that only God can do. Elaine offers words wrapped in encouragement, challenge, but most of all, hope. If you, or someone you know, is battling a terminal illness, this is a must read. You may just finish this book a little more encouraged than when you started."

Michelle S. Lazurek, Award winning author
of *Righteous and Lost*

"Terminal. In a moment, thoughts went from planning the next vacation to going away forever. Never coming back." If you can identify with these words, I'm so very sorry for your illness. But, I'm also grateful to be able to highly recommend Elaine W. Miller's new book *Praise the Lord and Pass the Chemo*. This resource will speak directly to your heart as Elaine shares wisdom learned from her own cancer journey — how it affects family, changes perspective, forces decisions. Above all, she urges a positive spirit that can thank God for everyday blessings. "No one chooses cancer. But we do choose how we respond." Believing music to be a healing balm, I was delighted with the hymns included in each chapter. Read this book for your own attitude adjustment, but then be sure to give away a copy to that friend who just received a scary diagnosis. She or he will thank you.

Lucinda Secrest McDowell
Author, *Ordinary Graces*

Praise the Lord and Pass the Chemo
Copyright © 2018 Elaine W. Miller

Published by EA Books Publishing a division of
Living Parables of Central Florida, Inc. a 501c3
EABooksPublishing.com

DEDICATION

Dedicated to
Cancer warriors and those who love them.
Life is worth living.
People are worth loving.
Smiles are worth smiling.
Laughter is gold.

CONTENTS

ACKNOWLEDGMENTS

With Praise and Thanksgiving

With praise to God who put a passion in my heart to write and trusted me to bring glory to Him through a cancer diagnosis. To Jesus who died so I could live forever. To the Holy Spirit who filled my heart with peace and these pages with words.

To my dearest husband, my lover, and my friend, my Dan: How I love being in love and living life with you. Thank you for your constant support. Thank you for loving me even more when my hair grew crazy and my body grew weary. What a blessing to know your care and never doubt your love.

To my children, Joanna and Bob, Elizabeth and Joe, and Sam and Katie: I know my cancer is harder on you than on me. Thank you for your love, your time, your concern. God blessed me with the best children. I am better because of you.

To my grandchildren, Gracie and Ryan; Connor, Garrett, Ava, Brenna, Charlotte, Isaac, Lucas, Gunnar, and one being knit; Lily and Jack: God hears a child's precious prayers. I am with you today because God heard your prayers for me. Wow! You are a powerful thirteen voices calling to God on my behalf. Pretty cool!

To my editor Dianne Barker: You poured your heart, your love, and your expertise into *Praise the Lord and Pass the Chemo* for the glory of God and for love of cancer patients in need of hope and joy. I will never forget the hours and days you worked to make our book shine.

To my writers group, Elizabeth Sliwa, Jill Printzenhoff, and Constance Buckley: Thank you for keeping me real and on target with the mission God gave me.

To Montrose Christian Writer's Conference: Here I learned the writing/publishing business and realized writing friendships dear to my heart. Thank you for teaching me, loving me, praying for me, and crowning me an Odd Duck. You helped me soar.

To the Advanced Writers and Speakers Association: My AWSA sisters pulled together with powerful prayers on my behalf. Really. You moved mountains for me.

To my prayer team, too numerous to name: What a precious gift you are to me. I call out to you and you call out to God on my behalf. Thank you for your sacrifice. Thank you for holding me in prayer when I feel too weak to stand alone.

To cancer patients: Thank you for blessing me with your love, your example, your willingness, and your openness to tell your stories so the world would know there is a hopeful response to this hard reality.

To my readers: All cancer journeys differ. Some in great sorrow; some with great joy. Some with hope; others hopeless. Wherever you are on this path, may the Lord be your strength. I am honored to call you friends and peers. We share a common cancer bond and will be joined forever. I thank God for you and pray *Praise the Lord and Pass the Chemo: A Hopeful Response to a Hard Reality* will bring joy to your days.

Chapter 1

Why Me, God?

*All the days ordained for me were written in your book
before one of them came to be* (Psalm 139:16b NIV).

"You have leukemia."

Too stunned to react, I sat silent. In a moment of a test result life had changed forever.

"For the glory of God," I said. Just being honest. That's what I said. Who knows what they will say when cancer rings the doorbell, and death's door moves next door. I didn't plan a speech for this moment because cancer happens to other people, not me. But it was me. Me and millions suffering in bodies sick with disease.

Many react to a cancer diagnosis asking, "Why me, God?"

Well, why not me? I've sat at the bedside of young mothers taking their last breaths. A powerful preacher was stricken during the prime of his God-ordained ministry. A little child played one day and collapsed the next. A newborn baby died before realizing life had more than pain to offer. Why them? Why not me? Questions humans will never answer.

"Why me?" We don't know why. But God knows. He is not standing in the distant heavens thinking, *How did that* happen? I had no idea my beloved child would have cancer. He knows. He cares. He loves us. He holds us. He promised.

Our cancer did not come as a shock to God. He knew before we were born that one day we would hear the word cancer.

On the day of my diagnosis, these words came to mind. ". . . All the days ordained for me were written in your book before one of them came to be" (Psalm 139:16b NIV). This day. This hard day. The day the doctor told me I had leukemia was written in God's book before I was born. In fact, Psalm 139 says this day was ordained for me.

Cancer ordained for me? For us?

"Ordain" is defined as "confer holy orders on" and "set apart for a purpose." Did God ordain this day and our future days of uncertainty, pain, drugs, and trauma to make us and our families holy? Did God confer a "holy order" on us to use our cancer for a purpose?

Instead of why me, perhaps we should ask, what now? If this is God's plan set apart for His purpose, how then shall we live the remaining years, months, days, and hours of our lives to know and fulfill that purpose?

Being angry at God, bitter at the world, wallowing in self sorrow, worrying about the future does no one any good, especially the cancer patient.

In the Bible we read of a man named Job, who had reason to ask God, "Why me?" God Himself tells us of Job, "There is no one on earth like him; he is blameless and upright, a man who fears God and shuns evil" (Job 1:8 NIV).

Being a good person promises no one a life free from pain. Job lost everything—his children, his servants, his animals, his wealth, and his health. Chapter 1 of his narrative concludes with, "In all this, Job did not sin by charging God with wrongdoing" (Job 1:22 NIV). He didn't get angry or ask God, "Why?"

Job's wife had a different reaction. "Are you still holding on to your integrity? Curse God and die!" (Job 2:9 NIV). Did her attitude change the circumstances or make matters better for herself or for her family? No. Cursing God helps no one.

Job's answer should ring in our hearts. ". . . Shall we accept good from God, and not trouble?" (Job 2: 10 NIV).

In the early days of dealing with my diagnosis, I wrote in my journal, "Why me? Because God trusts me to glorify Him in this." No other explanation made sense. God was honoring me with His trust that through my cancer I and others would see Jesus, be encouraged, receive hope, and learn to live and love more like Jesus.

God ordains each of our days for a purpose. Could there be a better life-purpose than to glorify Him?

Instead of throwing angry questions at God, let us accept God's purpose that we be holy, set apart, and filled with all the fruits of the spirit—love, joy, peace, patience, kindness, gentleness, self-control, goodness, and faithfulness. Isn't this how we want to spend our days? I know I do.

The life story of Joseph (the man with the coat of many colors as told in the book of Genesis) teaches us a strong truth. Joseph was his father's favorite son, so dad presented him with a beautiful multi-colored coat. Joseph's brothers were furious.

They neither possessed a fancy frock nor enjoyed the favor of their father, so they conceived a plot to rid their family of Joseph. The brothers threw him into a pit to die. Thinking murder may be a bit too harsh, they decided instead to sell him as a slave. Joseph was taken to a far-away land. His brothers returned home and convinced their father that Joseph was indeed dead.

Joseph's life continued on a downward spiral when he refused advances of the wife of Potiphar, one of Pharaoh's officials. Angry at Joseph's disinterest, Potiphar's wife falsely accused Joseph of a sexual attack. Joseph spent years in prison for a crime he did not commit. There he had time to fester over the betrayal of his brothers which ultimately lead to his imprisonment. Joseph never asked God, "Why me?" Instead, when freed from prison and reunited with his brothers, Joseph responded, "You intended to harm me, but God intended it for good to accomplish what is now being done" (Genesis 50:20 NIV).

We can see our cancer as Joseph saw his troubles. Cancer intends to harm us, but God intends it for good to accomplish His purpose in our lives for His glory.

"How do you feel?" friends often ask. I've pondered that query and decided my answer. "Surrendered. I feel surrendered." Surrendered to whatever God's will is for me. Surrendered to the knowledge that God has appointed for me a day to die. It may be sooner than I like, but selah—so be it. Surrendered to the pledge that however God answers prayers on my behalf, I will glorify Him. Surrendered to endure the pain as Christ endured the cross, for the joy set before Him and you and me. Oh, that wonderful joy set before us called Heaven!

As we walk together this road called cancer our souls will find solace and hope in music. I encourage singing or reading the precious promises found in the hymns. Singing brightens our spirits and keeps our eyes focused on joy rather than sorrow. When the days are low, lift up a song. Sing out and breathe in the precious truths and powerful promises of the old hymns.

"Take My Life, and Let It Be"
by Frances R. Havergal

Take my life and let it be consecrated, Lord, to thee.

Take my moments and my days.

Let them flow in ceaseless praise.

Let them flow in ceaseless praise.

Take my hands, and let them move

at the impulse of Thy love.

Take my feet, and let them be swift and beautiful for Thee.

Swift and beautiful for Thee.

Take my voice, and let me sing always only for my King.

Take my lips, and let them be

filled with messages from Thee.

Filled with messages from Thee.

Take my silver and my gold, not a mite would I withhold.

Take my intellect, and use

every power as Thou shalt choose.

Every power as Thou shalt choose.

Take my will, and make it Thine; it shall be no longer mine.

Take my heart; it is Thine own; it shall be Thy royal throne.

It shall be Thy royal throne.

Take my love; my Lord, I pour at Thy feet its treasure store.

Take myself, and I will be ever only, all for Thee.

Ever only, all for Thee.

Heavenly Father, You say to thank You for everything. So, I thank You for my cancer. Somehow in Your perfect plan for my life, You ordained these days for me and for my family. Teach us, Lord, all You would have us learn. Draw us close to You and hold my loved ones and me close when times are hard. Thank You, Lord, that You are acquainted with suffering. May we turn to You for comfort and joy. Use me, Lord, on this journey to shine for You. Bind satan, as I hold Your hand and choose to glorify You, learn more about You, and show the world what Jesus is like. God, You have ordained these days for me for Your glory. I know You hold me, You love me, You care about me, and You will never let me go. Thank You, my precious First Love. In Jesus' name I pray without ceasing. Amen.

Ribbons for Your Heart

Instead of asking, "Why me?" say, "Win Win!" We win when we surrender each day to the will of Jesus Christ. We win when we face challenges with confidence knowing Jesus holds us and He will never let us go. We win when we refuse to become bitter or angry. We win by living the rest of our lives with joy. We win by treasuring every moment of every day. We win by keeping our eyes on Jesus. And, we may even win by beating our friends and family in the race to Heaven. An abundant life on earth or an eternal life in Heaven is a win/win. Both sound wonderful to me. Wrap an *"I Win"* ribbon around your heart and surrender to God all the days He ordains for you.

Chapter 2

Laughing at Cancer

The Lord will fight for you; you need only to be still
(Exodus 14:14 NIV).

I don't want my obituary to read, "Elaine W. Miller lost her courageous battle with cancer. "I can't battle cancer! Woe is me if I spend my days putting on boxing gloves and slugging it out with a foe I cannot defeat. Battling cancer is a burden I refuse to bear.

Oncologists concur with what God said. "A cheerful heart is good medicine" (Proverbs 17:22 NIV). Laughter makes us better whether we are suffering with cancer or searching for lost car keys.

"You have cancer. Now, I want you to remove all stress from your life," my oncologist advised in all seriousness.

I laughed out loud. "Are you kidding me? You tell me I have cancer and say in your next sentence I am to remove all stress from my life. That's funny!" Perhaps my laughter was a defense against the shocking news my brain and emotions were trying to absorb. I could not make my cancer go away; but I could laugh away the stress of this disease.

The Cancer Treatment Centers of America (CTCA) offer Laughter Clubs to help cancer patients cope. I chuckled and wanted to sign up when I read what happens there. "One group exercise involves patients standing in a circle, with the leader in the middle. Patients put their fingertips on their cheekbones, chest or lower abdomen and make 'ha ha' or 'hee hee' sounds until they feel vibrations through their bodies . . . during these exercises, it is hard for people not to join in because laughter is so contagious . . . patients have said things like 'I didn't even think about cancer during Laughter Club' and 'That felt great! Things have been so hard that we hadn't laughed in months' . . . the 8-year-old daughter of a CTCA patient who attended Laughter Club said afterwards: 'I never thought about laughing every day, but now I realize I can. Like even when I don't feel happy, I can still laugh and feel better.'"[1]

Sounds fun, doesn't it? Cancer patients and their families need to have fun. Laughter is healthy. A belly laugh reduces stress, relaxes muscles, relieves pain, lowers blood pressure, and promotes well-being for the sick and for those who love them.

I remember fighting the daily parenting battle. Picking up toys, putting children to bed, then turning around to find more toys and kids not in their beds. Life can be exhausting on a good day. In tears, I called a friend who advised, "When you feel you can't take any more, just burst out laughing." I did. Laughing worked! Soon, everyone started laughing and life was bright again.

Laughter is contagious. When we laugh, people around us laugh and spirits lift from weary to worshipful. Cancer patients need to laugh and enjoy their families laughing with them. Isn't that how we want to be remembered? My children say when they think of my dad, the word *jolly* comes to mind. That's a legacy I hope lives on through me.

Of course, we must not neglect partnering with God and our doctors. We are responsible for the human decisions that help us defeat the enemy. Choices we make can extend the quantity and the quality of our lives. Choosing to eat healthy, exercise daily, obey our doctors, stay active, sleep well, avoid stress, and laugh are all proven cancer fighters.

But, in the ultimate battle for our lives and for our minds, let us never forget, "The Lord will fight for you. You need only to be still" (Exodus 14:14 NIV).

Deep in the night when life is quiet and our minds empty, satan (I never capitalize his name) attacks with worry, fear, loneliness, depression. Night terrors make us easy prey for satan's battle for our souls. In those times, resist satan and cling to the truth that God is fighting for us, and He always wins! Hallelujah!

God repeats His promise to fight for His children: ". . . the Lord your God fights for you, just as He promised. So be very careful to love the Lord your God" (Joshua 23:10-11 NIV). Could the key to stillness and confidence in this cancer battle lie in that last sentence? "So be very careful to love the Lord your God."

When sadness creeps in, let us focus our thoughts on Jesus and be very careful to love Him. How do we concentrate on loving the Lord? Rid our minds of the earthly and set our thoughts on the heavenly. Read the Psalms. Pray. Watch an inspirational movie. Surround ourselves with godly people. Take a walk and marvel at God's creation. Love God by loving neighbors with home-baked cookies. Do a good deed for someone who needs a heavenly touch. Whatever we do, let's love the Lord and keep laughing.

"Be still, and know that I am God . . ." (Psalm 46:10 NIV). God fights and wins battles humans never could. Be still. Know that He is God and we are not. Rest in Him. Live in stillness. Laugh.

The devil schemes to have us and our loved ones live in a house of gloom. Don't let the evil one win. There is victory in Jesus. Remember, God holds us, and He never lets us go. When we go off to sleep, He goes off to battle.

"The Lord is my strength and my shield; my heart trusts in Him, and He helps me. My heart leaps for joy, and with my song I praise Him" (Psalm 28:7 NIV). Like a child, laugh at the lyrics and sing this delightful song.

"I've Got the Joy, Joy, Joy"
by George Willis Cooke

I've got the joy, joy, joy, joy

Down in my heart (Where?)

Down in my heart (Where?)

Down in my heart.

I've got the joy, joy, joy, joy

Down in my heart. Down in my heart to stay.

And I'm so happy. So very happy

I have the love of Jesus in my heart (down in my heart).

And I'm so happy. So very happy

I have the love of Jesus in my heart.

[Subsequent lyrics include:]

I've got the peace that passes understanding

down in my heart . . .

I've got the far-out faith that freaks out the farmers

down in my heart . . .

I've got the glorious hope of my blessed redeemer way down in
the depths of my heart . . .

I've got the mighty Messiah that manifests miracles

down in the depths of my heart . . .

I've got the love of Jesus Christ my Savior

down in my heart . . .

I've got the wonderful love of my blessed redeemer

way down in the depths of my heart . . .

And if the devil doesn't like it he can sit on a tack.

Ouch! Sit on a tack . . .

I've got the infinite love of the living Lord

down in the depths of my heart . . .

I've got the love of Jesus, love of Jesus

down in my heart . . .

Heavenly Father, cancer is not a battle I ever wanted to fight. Thank You, Lord Jesus, for fighting for me. In the deep dark I cling to You as You go off to war on my behalf. Help me to rest in You and to be still when my mind races with worry and fear. Enable me to laugh when I feel like crying. Give me joy in this journey. May I be still and know, really know, and feel, and be totally aware that You are God, and I am not. I place my mind, my heart, my cancer, my family, my soul in You and I rest in the all-powerful, mighty, strong, able name of Jesus. Amen.

Ribbons for Your Heart

We can't fight cancer, but we can walk victoriously through this day. Our joy is not because of our circumstances, but because we have an eternal relationship with our Savior, Jesus Christ. Since our joy comes from the Holy Spirit and not by human effort, we can be like the Proverbs 31 woman who "laughs at days ahead." We have joy and giggles, rest and stillness   because God is fighting for us, and He never loses. Tie a *"Joy"* ribbon around your heart today and laugh!

Chapter 3

We Are All Terminal

Just as man is destined to die once, and after that to face judgment, so Christ was sacrificed once to take away the sins of many people; and he will appear a second time, not to bear sin, but to bring salvation to those who are waiting for Him (Hebrews 9:27-28 NIV).

"Is she saying I'm terminal?" I asked my dear hand-holding husband after the oncologist left the room.

Poor guy. Trying to comfort me and grasp his own grief, Dan said the only thing he could think, "Well, we're all terminal, aren't we?"

The genetic test results concluded, "low survivability, rapid progression, resistant to treatment." Sounded pretty terminal to me. My optimistic champion-of-a-husband encouraged me. "It says *low* survivability, not *no* survivability." But I found little blessing in his assessment.

Terminal. In a moment, thoughts went from planning the next vacation to going away forever. Never coming back. Funny, social media seemed to know before anyone else. Funeral home ads began popping up on my page.

Nothing hits you quite like a baseball-bat-smack-in-your-face diagnosis.

Thoughts of a long-ago prayer came to mind. "Do with me whatever You please." I'd surrendered my life to Jesus Christ. Now I could accept that whatever the outcome, my leukemia was what God pleased for His good purpose. He promised, "for it is God who works in you to will and to act according to His good purpose" (Philippians 2:13 NIV). If God is working in me through this leukemia, then my cancer is for God's good purpose. Who am I to doubt or to debate God?

We will all die someday. Only God knows when and how. . . a car crash . . . leukemia. God will do with us as He pleases. "Our God is in heaven; He does whatever pleases Him" (Psalm 115:3 NIV).

During the Viet Nam war, my husband served as a helicopter med evac corpsman. Once, when his helicopter was shot down, he survived injuries that could have been fatal. Another time, he happened to stand up in flight to prepare for landing and boarding wounded Marines. At that moment, a bullet shot up through the seat Dan had just left. By an instant, he escaped death. Our days are in God's hands. Death could come to us momentarily or years from now. The date and time is God's call, not ours.

Cancer gives us pause. The reality of our mortality looks us in the eye and asks, "So, do you know for sure, without a doubt, that when you die you will go to Heaven?" All of us, whether we have cancer or not, find comfort if we are certain of our final destination.

Here's my story:

Until mid-life I thought little of the after-life. By the world's standards I was a good girl. My goodness was good enough to win favor with a good God. Right? Until death stares us in the face, and we begin to wonder, *how good is good enough?*

Pregnant with my third child, I cringed when the doctor said, "Your pregnancy could be complicated. Perhaps you should consider an abortion." The obstetrician's words troubled me as I pondered my pregnancy. In my heart and mind, the fact that I even considered ending my baby's life proved I was not good enough for God.

My world fell apart. Fear of death consumed me. *This pregnancy could kill me!* I knew I would not go to Heaven.

"How *good* does one have to be to get into Heaven?" I asked a pastor, who told me wonderful news.

"The Bible says that no one is good," he said. "For all have sinned and fall short of the glory of God" (Romans 3:23 NIV). Some say they have never sinned. They haven't murdered or robbed anyone. They are good people. But sin is anything we do that displeases God. Gossip. Anger. Jealousy. Selfishness. We're all guilty of these things.

Further, I can prove we are all sinners. Do we teach our children to be bad? No. We teach them to be good. They know very well how to be bad. We are all sinners—separated from God from the day we are born. That isn't good news for us.

But the good news is God loves us. Because of our sin, we need a Savior. God provided that Savior in His own Son, Jesus Christ (the only person who is without sin). Jesus died on the cross, the sinless for the sinful, to pay the penalty for our sins.

"For Christ died for sins once for all, the righteous for the unrighteous, to bring you to God" (1 Peter 3:18).

Jesus was buried but three days later He rose again. The Bible says, "For God so loved the world that He gave His one and only Son, that whoever believes in Him shall not perish but have eternal life" (John 3:16 NIV).

Do you believe it?

Eight months pregnant, I stood at my kitchen window and prayed to God, "Dear Jesus, I can't do this without You. I am a sinner and I am sorry for my sins. I believe You died on the cross to take the punishment for my sin and that You rose on the third day. I give my life to You. Do with me whatever You please."

Well, He pleased to do a lot. Fear flew out the window and peace flew into my heart. I believed and knew that going to Heaven did not depend on my good works but on my belief in Jesus' death and resurrection.

A month later I was scheduled to have a c-section. Death was a possibility, but I had a peace I'd never known before. I would either have a baby or a home in Heaven. Either sounded wonderful to me. I thank God for His Son, Jesus; and I thank God for an uncomplicated delivery of a robust baby boy.

Jesus offers us an invitation. "Come to me all you who are weary and burdened, and I will give you rest" (Matthew 11:28 NIV).

Are you afraid of your diagnosis? Does death haunt you? Do you fear you aren't good enough to get to Heaven? Well, you aren't. Are you afraid you have sinned so terribly that God will never forgive you? Don't believe that lie. Jesus loves you.

There is nothing you have done that He will not forgive. Just ask Him.

Jesus says, "I tell you the truth, he who believes has everlasting life" (John 6:47 NIV). Come to Jesus now and be assured of your everlasting life in Heaven.

"Just as I Am"
by Charlotte Elliott

Just as I am, without one plea,
But that Thy blood was shed for me,
And that Thou bidd'st me come to Thee,
O Lamb of God, I come, I come!
Just as I am and waiting not
To rid my soul of one dark blot,
To Thee, whose blood can cleanse each spot,
O Lamb of God, I come, I come!
Just as I am, though tossed about
With many a conflict, many a doubt,
Fightings within, and fears without,
O Lamb of God, I come, I come!
Just as I am, Thou wilt receive,
Wilt welcome, pardon, cleanse, relieve;
Because Thy promise I believe,
O Lamb of God, I come, I come!
Just as I am, Thy love unknown
Hath broken every barrier down;
Now, to be Thine, yea, Thine alone,
O Lamb of God, I come, I come!

Heavenly Father, thank You that we can know we are going to Heaven to live eternally with You. What joy fills our hearts as we trust in You and not in our own insufficient good works. Holy Spirit, enter the hearts of those living in fear and uncertainty of their destination and nudge them to pray to You this prayer of salvation:

Heavenly Father, I am a sinner. Thank You for sending Your perfect Son, Jesus Christ to die for my sin. Thank You, Jesus Christ, for taking the punishment I deserve. Forgive me, Lord. I am so sorry for my sin. I believe you died, and three days later You rose again. I believe Jesus Christ is my Lord and my Savior and I give my life to Him. Come into my heart, Lord Jesus. Fill me with Yourself and take away my fears and uncertainties. Oh, Lamb of God, I come, I come! Amen.

Ribbons for Your Heart

The beauty of cancer research is that every day brings a new discovery. Shortly after my "low-survivability" diagnosis, a new drug was approved for treatment of my "high-risk" leukemia. One pill daily (and God) stopped the progression of my cancer, giving me hope for many years of joyful living. Reality: one day our bodies will stop breathing and we will meet the Lord. Are you ready? I hope so. If you're unsure, pray the prayer that follows the hymn and tie a *"Going to Heaven"* ribbon around your heart.

Chapter 4

Praise the Lord and Pass the Chemo

But I have raised you up for this very purpose, that I might show you My power and that My name might be proclaimed in all the earth (Exodus 9:16 NIV).

"I have a praise report! I have cancer!" George smiled wide as he announced his diagnosis to a group gathered for a Wednesday night of prayer.

"George! How is that a praise report?" The stunned assembly seemed to ask in unison.

"Can you imagine the people I'll meet and tell about Jesus? Doctors! Nurses! All kinds of medical staff! Why, I'm having chemotherapy every week with the same seven people in the same room. I'm going to tell all of them 'I know I'm going to Heaven. Do you?' And they won't be able to leave because we're all having chemo."

For George, cancer was a reason for thanksgiving. Telling people about Jesus was his passion. Cancer opened doors to share his faith with people he otherwise might never meet.

I would have loved being in the doctor's office when the oncologist tried to heal George, and George tried to heal the oncologist.

"George, this is serious. You are a sick man."

"Doctor, if you don't know Jesus as your Savior, you are a lot sicker than I am!"

Remembering my God-loving friend, I determined—like George—to look at cancer as an opportunity rather than an obstacle.

When Moses was threatened by plagues, God assured him, "But I have raised you up for this very purpose, that I might show you my power and that my name might be proclaimed in all the earth" (Exodus 9:16 NIV).

God did not make a mistake when He placed Moses in the desert or us at the cancer center, laboratory, waiting room, or infusion center. This moment—meeting these doctors, nurses, fellow cancer patients—isn't a surprise to God. He raised us up for His purpose to show His power that His name be proclaimed. Sounds like a *Hallelujah* moment to me!

Having determined to see cancer as an opportunity to love and serve Jesus, I walked into the cancer center with joy in my step and a prayer in my heart.

Every six weeks I receive a five-hour infusion in a private room with one nurse—what an opportunity to make a friend I may have never met, except for cancer. On my first infusion day the nurse and I talked about Jesus. She shared about her marriage. Nothing serious. Just the everyday struggles of loving your man while working fulltime and rearing children. Of course, I told her about my book, *We All Married Idiots*. She laughed, agreed with the title, and ordered my book.

"You must be tired of listening to me." I smiled as the sedative kicked in. My eyes and tongue grew heavy.

"Oh, no! I could listen to you all day." She meant it. Without a hint of flattery or a nurse's bedside manners, she spoke with sincerity as the Holy Spirit worked in her heart.

Later, with a hop and a skip, I left the hospital thanking George for his example and God for allowing me to share Jesus and hope with a new friend. Exhilarated by all God did that day, I got into my car proclaiming, "Well, praise the Lord and pass the chemo!"

No one chooses cancer. Those lousy test results aren't our idea. But we do choose how we respond. What good does sulking do? Let's replace sad thoughts with songs of praise. Ask, allow, and expect God to use this illness for His purpose, to show God's power, so His name will be proclaimed wherever our cancer journey leads us.

Singing songs of praise does more toward a cure than words of doom. Fanny Crosby, blinded before her first birthday, and the author of over 5,000 hymns, chose an attitude of praise. She said, "It seemed intended by the blessed providence of God that I should be blind all my life, and I thank him for the dispensation. If perfect earthly sight were offered me tomorrow I would not accept it. I might not have sung hymns to the praise of God if I had been distracted by the beautiful and interesting things about me."[2] Don't be distracted. Keep your eyes on Jesus and sing.

"Praise Him! Praise Him!"
by Fanny J. Crosby

Praise Him! Praise Him! Jesus our blessed Redeemer!
Sing, O earth; His wonderful love proclaim!
Hail Him! Hail Him! Highest archangels in glory;
Strength and honor give to His holy name!
Like a shepherd Jesus will guard His children;
In His arms He carries them all day long.
Praise Him! Praise Him! Tell of His excellent greatness;
Praise Him! Praise Him, ever in joyful song!
Praise Him! Praise Him! Jesus, our blessed Redeemer!
For our sins He suffered and bled, and died;
He our rock, our hope of eternal salvation;
Hail Him! Hail Him! Jesus, the crucified.
Sound His praises — Jesus who bore our sorrows;
Love unbounded, wonderful, deep, and strong!
Praise Him! Praise Him! Tell of His excellent greatness;
Praise Him! Praise Him, ever in joyful song!
Praise Him! Praise Him! Jesus our blessed Redeemer!
Heavenly portals loud with hosannas ring.
Jesus, Saviour, reigneth forever and ever;
Crown Him! Crown Him! Prophet, and Priest, and King!
Christ is coming, over the world victorious;
Power and glory unto the Lord belong.
Praise Him! Praise Him! Tell of His excellent greatness;
Praise Him! Praise Him, ever in joyful song!

Heavenly Father, I praise You because I have cancer. Thank You for the opportunity this disease gives me to share hope and faith with the hopeless and the faithless who experience the horrors of this illness, but have never known the majesty of You. I pray I will do this disease well. Strengthen me to live these days full of hope and joy. Fill me with Your Holy Spirit that I may show love, joy, peace, and patience to my new world of friends who hurt. Be Lord of my mouth, that I may open it for You. Be Lord of my eyes, that I will see people as You see them. Be Lord of my heart, that I will love people as You love them. Through all these days, give me a heart and voice of praise. In Jesus' name, amen.

Ribbons for Your Heart

Hannah Whitall Smith, author of *The Christian's Secret of a Happy Life*, writes, "When your trial comes, then, put it right into the will of God, and climb into that will as a child climbs into its mother's arms."[3] Let Fanny Crosby, Hannah Whitall Smith, and my friend George be our models of courage today. They all knew the benefits of praising God, trusting Him, and being used by Him in the worst of circumstances. Praise is a choice. Choose wisely, and wrap a *"Praise the Lord"* ribbon around your heart.

Chapter 5

Time Is Short—Legacy Is Long

Train a child in the way he should go, and when he is old he will not turn from it (Proverbs 22:6 NIV).

Her beauty stood out more than her baldness. We didn't speak, and I didn't stare. Without a word, she touched my heart. Sitting in the airport terminal, I wrote in my journal, "A true beauty is one whose features are so fine that she retains her loveliness even when her hair is gone."

Sad. So young.

Nestled in my assigned seat, I hoped whoever sat next to me on the flight would sleep for the next three hours for I had a manuscript to edit. I had work to do.

Sweet, bald-headed beauty stopped at my row and slid into her seat. I was quick to keep my eyes on the papers scattered in front of me.

"Hi. My name is Paige. Are you writing a book?"

And so, our three-hour conversation began.

She had cancer. Deadly. And three children. Lively.

Eager to talk, she shared how her life and parenting changed when she learned she had little time left to influence the hearts of her children. I asked Paige if I could share her words of wisdom. She smiled and gave permission. In Paige's own words:

- "Meaningful moments will replace materialism as the goal for the day."
- "Attending family celebrations will be a priority."
- "My children are no longer my world. Instead, I want to show the world to my children."
- "Teach my children that life is about real people who need real people—not about video games and the latest toys."
- "Grow compassion in the hearts of my children by showing them the hurting in the world."
- "Grow my children to be kind instead of selfish."
- "Grow my children to care more about people than possessions."
- "Teach my children they are on this earth to be angels—messengers from God."

Paige described how cancer had changed her life:

"My days of selfishness—of materialism—are gone and my life of giving back has begun. Cancer is a gift that changed my thinking from *let's see how many toys I can accumulate to let's see how many lives I can touch before I die.*"

I'm thankful Paige touched my life. I hope she touched yours.

Whether we live long or short, we want to have a positive impact on our families. A cancer diagnosis gives us pause to realize our time to leave a legacy is brief. Most parents don't have that cancer pause and, therefore, may never grab the moments all moms and dads have to influence their children.

We can be so busy living life, we miss teaching our little ones how life should be lived.

We may not have tomorrow. But we have today. Don't waste it. Our children won't remember the price tag on the latest toy. But, they will remember the priceless moments we spend with them. Go outside and create memories in God's playground. It's free. Take a walk together. Pick flowers. Pare apples. Make up stories. Read a book. Bake cookies. Cuddle. Hug. Kiss. Sing. Laugh. Pray. Lots of little moments make loads of big memories.

My fifth-grade teacher left an imprint on my life. Mrs. Harrod began each day with our class in singing, "I Would Be True." Nearly fifty years later, the words still ring in my heart—her legacy to me.

"I Would Be True"
by Howard Walter

I would be true, for there are those who trust me;
I would be pure, for there are those who care;
I would be strong, for there is much to suffer;
I would be brave, for there is much to dare;

I would be friend of all — the foe, the friendless;
I would be giving, and forget the gift;
I would be humble, for I know my weakness;
I would look up, and laugh, and love and lift.

I would be faithful through each passing moment;
I would be constantly in touch with God;
I would be strong to follow where He leads me;
I would have faith to keep the path Christ trod;

Heavenly Father, You tell us to train up a child in the way he should go, and when he is old he will not depart from it. I may have little time to train my child. But I have today. May I use this day well to leave a legacy. To teach my precious child about You. Strengthen me to parent well, to smile, to enjoy the moments, to treasure the simple, to laugh, and to love. And should the day come when I can no longer draw them to my heart, I thank You, Heavenly Father, for parenting them. Hold them close, Lord. Guide them. Protect them. Surround them with Your angels. Thank You, Lord, that You love them even more than I do. I give my little ones to You, knowing You are the perfect parent. Thank You for caring for them when I cannot. In Jesus' name, amen.

Ribbons for Your Heart

Paige Hilfer was born on December 18, 1967 and died on March 22, 2012 at the age of forty-four. So few years, but so great a legacy. Although her children may forget the feel of her hair, they will remember her smile, her love, her teaching, and the way she lived life. Time is short for all of us even if we live long. Seize your days and your opportunities to show your little ones how to look up, laugh, love, and live while you tie a *"Leave a Legacy"* ribbon around your heart.

Chapter 6

Angels Without Wings

*The angel of the Lord encamps around those who fear him,
and he delivers them* (Psalm 34:7 NIV).

"What do you want to be when you grow up?"

"Grandma, when I grow up I want to be an angel!!!" my
grandson proclaimed with bright eyes, a huge smile, and three
exclamation points. What five-year-old says such a thing?

Taken aback, I wondered. *What does an angel do?* My trusty
Webster's defines angel as, "a messenger from God."[4] Wow!
Isn't that what God asks all of us to be? We are His messengers
to a world in need of an angel's touch. What a great goal!

Still, I wondered. *What does an angel do in the normal day-to-
day?* Psalm 34:7 says, "The angel of the Lord encamps around
those who fear him, and he delivers them."

Angels can be in heavenly form. Ministering spirits we
cannot see or touch soothe and comfort and give us peace and
rest.

Angels can also appear in human form—people who arrive
without notice or in answer to prayer, to fulfill a physical,

emotional, or spiritual need. God places people in our lives as His messengers of comfort and care.

Have you ever been in so much pain you couldn't move or speak? Years ago, I had complications after major surgery. Unable to communicate, but with my mind racing, I thought, *I am going to die. No one can be in this much pain and survive.* A sheet of white coats surrounded my bed. Doctors and nurses were prodding and poking. Every touch was agonizing. Except one.

Her every touch was comfort. She sat cradling my head in her soft arms. When the circle of white coats left, she stayed. You might say she "encamped around me." Throughout the long, awful night she held me, her kind eyes smiling, her lips repeating, "You are going to be all right." In the morning my pain was tolerable, and the nurse stationed at my head had gone home. Or, so I thought.

Hoping to thank this sweet one for her tender care, I searched the eyes of every nurse who checked on me throughout my week-long hospital stay. But my nurse did not return. *She must have gone on vacation*, I assumed. Wanting to send her a note, I asked my other nurses for her name and address.

"What nurse? No nurse stayed with you throughout the night." The hospital staff had no idea who this person might be. So, I asked my husband. He never left me. Surely, he saw her. He confirmed, "I don't know who you're talking about. There was no nurse holding your head."

Was she an angel? I'll let you decide.

"Angels without wings" is the term my friend called the people God placed at her side during her cancer journey. Paige shared how these wingless angels softened her heart and strengthened her faith in God:

"I was such a selfish person. Then cancer hit, and the angels arrived. I decided to stop concentrating on my circumstances and learn how I could give back so much that was given to me."

Paige spoke of the human angels in her life:

- "Angels showed up daily at my door."
- "An angel handed me his airline ticket when he saw I was sick and there was no seat for me on the airplane."
- "Angels blessed me with weeks of prepared meals and child care."
- "Angels gave $20,000 to help with my medical expenses."

Yes, God sends His ministering spirits to help us through difficult days. He knows and cares that we have cancer. He has not left us without aid. God sees every need and meets it, in His way, in His time.

When cancer brings you low, look up and see your angels without wings.

God never intended we make this journey alone. Be willing to let people help us, love us, cry with us, pray for us, cut our grass, do our laundry, watch our children, sit with us, take us to the doctor . . . Now is the time to realize when we allow people into our lives, we are blessing them as they bless us because they are doing the work of God.

Paige added me to her list of angels without wings. Why? What did I do? We were together for a short three-hour airplane ride. Paige said, "You listened. You let me talk. You cared. You prayed." How simple it is to be an angel.

Many years ago, my neighbor and I were thrilled that both of us were expecting our third child. We envisioned our little boys playing together and becoming lifelong friends. Midway through her pregnancy, Cindy sat on my couch with the news. She had breast cancer. Numb. Speechless. We fell into each other's arms and wept. It wasn't the time for talk. It was a moment to mourn. Cindy thanked me for my hugs and tears and said, "You've been an angel to me today."

Sometimes all we can do is weep and pray, and that is enough.

"Every generous act and every perfect gift is from above, coming from the Father of Heavenly lights" (James 1:17). Look for the gifts coming down to us from the Father. Let's surround ourselves with people of light and allow the angels into our lives, knowing it is God Himself Who sent them to us.

What if angels come by day, but by night demons fill our minds? Where are the angels then? Be assured, the angels and God are encamped around us, especially in the darkness.

A young mother with five little ones received the dreaded diagnosis. Our church went into "angels-without-wings" mode. Meals and help arrived every day, but God's plan for me was not in the kitchen.

Instead, God led me to a prayer ministry for her. On my knees night after night, interceding for this dear woman was my calling. Who knows the impact of those prayers? I don't know if she fell into deep, pain-free sleep or if my prayers eased her night-time worries. I do know that God often woke me to pray for her long hours throughout the night.

If we feel the midnight terrors, don't focus on the fears but on the angels encamped around our bedside, knowing that God stirred someone, somewhere, to pray for us in our sleeplessness.

Let's sing our sorrows away whether the sun or the stars are shining, trusting in the truth of this spiritual:

"All Night, All Day"
by Otis L. McCoy

All night, all day,

Angels watching over me, my Lord

All night, all day,

Angels watching over me.

Now I lay me down to sleep

Angels watching over me, my Lord.

Pray the Lord my soul to keep.

Angels watching over me.

All night, all day,

Angels watching over me, my Lord.

All night, all day,

Angels watching over me.

Lord, stay with me through the night.

Angels watching over me, my Lord.

Wake me with the morning light.

Angels watching over me.

All night, all day,

Angels watching over me, my Lord.

All night, all day,

Angels watching over me.

Heavenly Father, thank You for the angels You send to meet my every need. Keep me from discouragement or fear. Open my eyes to Your provision and goodness and cast out my pride and my self-sufficiency. I can't do this cancer alone. I need You, God, and I need Your angels. I pray in Jesus' name that You will make me an angel. Open my eyes to those in need of prayer. Show me ways I can be a messenger from God to others. Make me a blessing to the angels You send my way. Thank You for the prayers on my behalf and Your sweet answer to each one. I know You are with me. You promise to never leave me. I have nothing to fear as I listen for the angel wings surrounding me. What sweet peace You bring, dear Holy Spirit. I ask You to stay and cradle my head in the light and in the dark in Jesus' name, amen.

Ribbons for Your Heart

"God be with me in this journey" is a prayer we never have to pray. He promises, "Never will I leave you; never will I forsake you" (Hebrews 13:5 NIV). He holds us, loves us, and cares for us, even when we think He has left us. I assure you He did not. His angels encamp around us in heavenly and in human form. Tie an *"Angels Watching Over Me"* ribbon around your heart and rejoice!

Chapter 7

The Worst of Times—A Child Has Cancer

*Have I not commanded you? Be strong and courageous. Do
not be terrified; do not be discouraged, for the Lord your God
will be with you wherever you go*
(Joshua 1:9 NIV).

Two thoughts came to mind when I heard my diagnosis.
First, *for the glory of God.* Second, *I'm thankful I have cancer and
not one of my children.*

Having cancer takes courage. Watching your child suffer
takes surrender.

I've sat with mothers at the bedside of their sick little ones
and marveled as the peace and presence of God filled the
hospital room. The strength and joy they experienced while
living the most horrendous of every mother's nightmare
revealed a power that only comes from God.

"How did you stay so strong?" I asked a sweet mother
whose baby boy died before he was one week old. Here's her
story:

"Losing Josh was difficult. Heart wrenching. Mind-
numbingly painful. But the Lord poured out His peace on me. I
was given a peace that transcends all understanding. I had

never felt that kind of peace. There is nothing like it. It is a protective covering. My time with Josh was a time in my life when Christ was so close that I could feel Him. But losing Josh was difficult."

She held her son a short six days. As we sat together, I witnessed a woman in total surrender to Christ and His plan for her and her newborn. The presence of God in the neo-natal intensive care unit was undeniable. Unseen angels surrounded mother and child as God held them both in His strong and loving arms.

"God is teaching me so much through Joshua's life," she stated while he lived, and then repeated after he died.

"What did God teach you during the most difficult time of your life?" I asked.

Observing and listening to my friend, I learned when we are without strength, we are strongest. When we have nothing in ourselves to hold on to, we cling to the cross and the resurrected power of Christ. Jesus is all we have, and He is all we need.

Joshua's mother shared six life-lessons we can all follow when treading life's deep waters:

1. Seek God Immediately.

Don't question God's will. Don't ask God, "Why?" Simply seek Him. Don't seek him for answers. Seek His presence.

God promises, "'You will seek me and find me when you seek me with all your heart. I will be found by you,' declares the Lord . . ." (Jeremiah 29:13-14 NIV). The answers to our difficult questions may not be forthcoming, but God Himself will be found. And He is enough.

How do we seek God? Through reading the Bible and praying to God — the One Who created our children and loves them the most.

Seeking God keeps us from being tossed to and fro with fears and fretfulness. When we seek Him, our rapid heart-rates calm as He holds us and our babies close.

A mother whose three-year-old son was dying wrote to me of the peace she experienced when she sought God. For years she watched her baby's cancer escalate and his body deteriorate. Pleading with her son to keep fighting, to not give up, she grew weary of words. Silently, she stopped fighting and sought God. Her Bible opened to these words, "The Lord will fight for you; you need only to be still" (Exodus 14:14 NIV). Calm came over her as she surrendered her son and herself to the will of her Heavenly Father.

Don't wait! Seek God immediately. We can't cure cancer or heal this disease in our own strength. We need God. Now. Not after we've tried every other remedy to relieve the pain. We'll grow tired. As well, our loud complaining may keep us from hearing God's whisper to our hearts.

2. Surrender to God's Will Unconditionally.

Don't make deals with God. God doesn't want to give us a bargain. He wants to give us Himself. He doesn't want our emotionally-driven promises, He wants our whole hearts and our total trust.

Acknowledge His power to heal or not to heal our bodies. Surrender to Him, praying   the prayer Jesus taught us to pray, "Thy will be done." Then, we will know the peace of the mother who surrendered her child to God saying, "My son belongs to You, God. He isn't mine to keep. I know You love my boy even more than I do. Trusting You to do what is best, I give my child to You, Heavenly Father. Your will be done."

3. Obey God Absolutely.

Ask God every day for wisdom and guidance and follow His leading every step of the way. God exhorts us, "Do not let this Book of the Law depart from your mouth; meditate on it day and night, so that you may be careful to do everything written in it" (Joshua 1:8 NIV). If ever there is a time to meditate on God's Word day and night and obey what He says, the time is now.

The Bible is filled with encouraging words that lift us out of the doldrums of the cancer culture. As well, only the Bible gives us divine direction for living a victorious life, especially when we feel defeated.

Why not choose a life verse or a cancer verse to meditate on? My life verse is, "Let us fix our eyes on Jesus, the author and perfecter of our faith, who for the joy set before him endured the cross, scorning its shame, and sat down at the right hand of the throne of God. Consider him who endured such opposition from sinful men, so that you will not grow weary and lose heart" (Hebrews 12:2-3). Whenever I am afraid or in a difficult dilemma, I focus on Jesus instead of the fear or the dilemma. When we seek God and ask Him, He will lead us to verses we can cling to when we feel like there is nothing left to hold on to.

We can't obey God if we don't know what He says, so let's be students of His Word. The Bible is filled with God's precious promises. How will we know them unless we read them? Be alert to listen and quick to obey what He tells us to do.

4. Trust God Patiently.

Patience is a virtue, but it's not mine. Patience is also a fruit of the Holy Spirit. We who know Christ as our Savior should be patient people. But we fail, don't we? We humans want our way and we want our way now! Trusting God can be a challenge when we battle impatience.

I remember the day I became impatient with God to fix my problems and fix them immediately. I'd grown weary of praying. God didn't seem to be listening, and I wasn't hearing from Him. Frustrated, I decided to seek God in His Word. Not knowing where to look for answers, I randomly (so I thought) flipped open the Bible to Isaiah. There was God's answer to me. "'For my thoughts are not your thoughts, neither are your ways my ways,' declares the Lord. 'As the heavens are higher than the earth, so are my ways higher than your ways and my thoughts than your thoughts. As the rain and the snow come down from heaven, and do not return to it without watering the earth and making it bud and flourish, so that it yields seed for the sower and bread for the eater, so is my word that goes out from my mouth; It will not return to me empty, but will accomplish what I desire and achieve the purpose for which I sent it. You will go out in joy and be led forth in peace'" (Isaiah 55:8-12 NIV). What a confirmation that God will accomplish and achieve His purpose in our lives, which will bring us joy and peace. I can trust Him to fulfill that promise. You can, too.

God's timetable is not our timetable. We need to be patient and trust that He knows our troubles and is working through them in His time. God sees the beginning, the middle, and the end of this train wreck called cancer. We may only see the dark in the midst. Wait and rely on God to work as He brings us to the end light. Waiting is hard, but God has a plan, and His plan is perfect and good. Trust God and be patient. Watch in awe as He achieves His purpose and accomplishes His desire through this difficulty, knowing we will go out with joy and be led forth in peace. What a precious promise!

5. Accept God's Plan Completely.

We can't change God's plan and will only become frustrated if we try. Anger, bitterness, and blame accomplish nothing good. Rather, those feelings fertilize rotting roots in our hearts, rob us of peace, steal our joy, and deprive us of abundant days with our loved ones.

Cancer is not God's punishment, but cancer is His plan for us. God didn't cause our cancer, but God allowed our cancer. For reasons we don't understand—and we may never know why—God chose our families and trusted us to glorify Him through this disease. We can live in victory when we accept God's plan completely, watch for God's miracles, listen to the lessons He teaches, and live alert to the people He puts in our paths to love.

A father said through his son's death, he and his wife had opportunities to comfort and pray for other parents with cancer-stricken children. In cancer center waiting rooms and hospitals, this truth is lived out. "Praise be to the God and Father of our Lord Jesus Christ, the Father of compassion and the God of all comfort, who comforts us in all our troubles, so that we can comfort those in any trouble with the comfort we ourselves have received from God" (2 Corinthians 1:3-4 NIV).

We can choose to feel honored to be a cancer family, for God chose us to suffer, to become more like Christ, and to ". . . follow in his steps" (1 Peter 2:21 NIV). In accepting God's plan completely, we acknowledge that God has a higher purpose in our pain. Through our suffering, God uses us to accomplish His plan on earth.

God does the same for our children, so innocent, yet afflicted with a devastating disease. As parents, our best choice is to cling to Jesus while accepting God's plan as good. Any other option (drinking, hating, denying) does no good. Only God's plan is good. When we accept God's plan, we teach our children to accept His will and plan for them as well. Watching us draw near to God, our children will, too.

God promises to hold our suffering babies close to His heart. Angels we do not see (or maybe we do) hover over and around our precious ones. Jesus, the Good Shepherd, enfolds His little lambs. What peace we have knowing Jesus loves our children even more than we do. He is the perfect parent. He sees each one created by Him. God knows and cares that our babies have cancer. With grace and love He will accomplish His will for their lives and ours.

Three-year-old Bobby was beginning his chemotherapy. Doctors warned his parents the chemo would rage and Bobby would suffer. "He will be so sick you will think he is dying," his oncologist said. The dreaded day arrived, and many people prayed. The chemotherapy was administered while Bobby smiled and read his books. His parents waited for the forewarned sickness, which never arrived. Bobby sat eating cereal while watching his favorite television show without a hint that he was supposed to look like he was dying. Suffering was not God's plan for Bobby's life.

Although Bobby did not suffer, not every child shares this happy tale. My baby brother ravaged red from radiation treatments. So burned, he must have hurt all over. Yet, he demonstrated an acceptance many adults would have difficulty achieving. Children trust in ways their parents may not. Witnessing their parents' trust in God, the little ones trust God, too.

A child was born with disease. With peace and confidence the new mother proclaimed, "My baby is God's good and perfect gift. God was in control on day one. I know God is in control of this."

We know our children are God's good and perfect gifts. We can accept God's plan unconditionally because God is in control and His plan is good and perfect.

Jesus the Son accepted God the Father's plan for Him by dying on the cross for our sins. No one understood at the time of the crucifixion, but God had a plan and a purpose when Jesus died and rose three days later. In the same way, God has a plan and a purpose for our families, even when we don't understand the why.

6. Thank God Continually.

Thanking God continually is a challenge we need to obey. In our quest to obey God absolutely, we are to "give thanks in all circumstances, for this is God's will for you in Christ Jesus"

(1 Thessalonians 5:18 NIV). When God uses absolutes like *all circumstances*, He means *all circumstances*.

How can we—and why should we—thank God a child has cancer? Well, what is the alternative? A bitter, angry, pain-filled spirit? Mama crying all day or being angry or bitter are memories we do not want for our children. Be aware that more than cancer scars can develop when a child doesn't understand why mommy and daddy are crying or angry. Your precious little one may think cancer is his fault, and that he is responsible for making mommy so sad and daddy so angry.

Thanking God continually can turn a gloomy day to a glorious one. As cancer brings torment, so thankfulness brings relief. Whether our days are filled with hope or dread, we live them best when we choose to thank our Heavenly Father.

There are medical benefits to thanking God. During uncomfortable treatments and tests, thanksgiving boosts our spirits and aids in healing our bodies and our minds. I've realized that when I pray and thank God, my body relaxes and pain decreases.

There are mental benefits to thanking God. Keeping a journal of our thoughts, our prayers, and our blessings will make these cancer days brighter. Writing works as therapy to our broken spirits.

For the sake of our children, and in obedience to God, we must thank God continually. Our children will be lifted up, our spirits will be blessed, and our God will be glorified.

Practice these principles gleaned from a mother whose baby died. She went through the worst and learned that the best is to seek God, surrender to God, obey God, trust God, accept God's plan, and thank God. Don't wait to live these principles. Embrace them immediately, unconditionally, absolutely, patiently, completely, and continually.

I've added one more principle.

7. Sing to Jesus Joyfully.

Singing shows we do seek, surrender, obey, trust, accept, and thank God. Sing as a prayer of surrender to Jesus:

"Have Thine Own Way, Lord!"
by Adelaide A. Pollard

Have Thine own way, Lord! Have Thine own way!
Thou art the Potter, I am the clay.
Mold me and make me after Thy will,
While I am waiting yielded and still.
Have Thine own way, Lord! Have Thine own way!
Search me and try me, Master, today!
Whiter than snow, Lord, wash me just now,
As in Thy presence humbly I bow.
Have Thine own way, Lord! Have Thine own way!
Wounded and weary, help me I pray!
Power — all power — surely is Thine!
Touch me and heal me, Savior divine!
Have Thine own way, Lord! Have Thine own way!
Hold o'er my being absolute sway!
Fill with Thy Spirit till all shall see
Christ only, always, living in me!

Heavenly Father, this shouldn't be hard to pray, but my heart is stubborn and sad as I fall before You in surrender and ask for Your will, and not my will in my life and the life of my loved one who carries cancer. Of course, I pray for total healing. Lord, I know that is my will and I know that is Your will, too. But, we may think differently on how to reach that goal. I realize You may see total healing happening in Heaven. I'm not ready to give my child to You, but I know I must. You have a perfect plan for my family and for me. May I trust You completely wherever Your will takes us. Thank You for carrying us close to Your heart as You lead and as we follow our sweet Shepherd, Jesus Christ. I surrender to You. Thy will be done in Jesus' name, amen.

Ribbons for Your Heart

Be still knowing the Lord is fighting for you. While He goes off to battle, stay calm and practice the following disciplines: 1. Seek God immediately—don't wait until you've tried every doctor and remedy available. 2. Surrender to God unconditionally—don't bargain with God. 3. Obey God absolutely—obeying partially is not obedience. 4. Trust God patiently—God's timetable is the best timetable. 5. Accept God's plan completely—what good will it do if you don't? 6. Thank God continually—give God the glory no matter His plan for your life. 7. Sing to Jesus joyfully—and you'll put a song in your child's heart. To reverence His authority, tie a *"Surrendered"* ribbon around your heart and let God do the rest!

Chapter 8

Christ Is the Big C

I have been crucified with Christ; and I no longer live, but Christ lives in me (Galatians 2:20 NIV).

Cancer is not the big *c*. Christ is the big *C*.

Drives me nuts! All the negativity about cancer. We claim Jesus won the victory in our lives, and then we add, "but we have the big C." You bet we do. Whether we survive or die, Christ is our big C. Christ, not cancer, holds our lives in His hands.

I remember as a little girl hearing for the first time the dreaded *c* word. After a telephone conversation with my grandmother, my mother burst into sobs. I ran to comfort her.

"What's wrong?"

In a voice I could hardly hear, my petite mother whispered, "C. Uncle Bill may have *c*."

"I don't know what *c* is. What is *c*?"

Unable to speak the word out loud, my mother gave me a new clue. "*C-a*. You know. *C-a*." My mother barely whimpered the first two letters of the unmentionable *c*-word.

"Cancer?" I said in my not-so-petite voice.

"Sh-h-h-h-h. Yes." Mom cried and whispered her disapproval that I would ever say that awful word out loud.

The happy news is my uncle did not have cancer. No doubt his diagnosis would have been the same whether Mom referred to his illness as *c* or she—horror of horrors—added the *a-n-c-e-r*.

Why is it so hard for us to say this word? Why do we fear naming our disease?

A woman wrote a glowing "hallelujah" for her cancer healing. She attributed her survival to the fact that she never once spoke the word, *cancer*. Even better, she permitted no one in her presence or in her home to refer to her illness as *cancer*. She believed the mere mention of *cancer* would somehow hamper God's healing touch. Really? Remember, our God is omnipotent, all-powerful. Nothing can limit Him.

Is cancer more powerful than Christ?

I have blood cancer. I can spend my days feeling miserable knowing my blood is bad, or I can dwell in the reality and the truth that I belong to Christ. Whether my blood is healthy or ravaged by leukemia cells, God says my blood is precious. "He will rescue them from oppression and violence, for precious is their blood in his sight" (Psalm 72:14 NIV). Wow! My blood is precious to God for Christ lives in me. He flows through my veins. He is my big C!

Don't make cancer your idol. Christ is God. Cancer is not. Stop worshipping this disease by living in fear that cancer has more power than Christ.

If we let cancer replace Christ as our big C, our hearts may become bitter, or angry, or depressed, or anxious, or afraid, or all of these. But when Christ takes His rightful place in our hearts, He fills us with His love, joy, peace, trust, and hope. So when the doubts and anxieties arise—and they will—let us remember who is the big C in our lives. Focus on Christ, not cancer.

We don't know God's plan, the doors of ministry He wants to open to us, the books He wants us to write, or those He will put in our path to encourage and pray for at the grocery store or cancer center. Be watchful for His hand and be on the lookout for His angels. If we focus on cancer and not on Christ, we may not redeem this time for the glory of God. We'll just worry and waste away.

There's a daily battle going on in our bodies and in our minds. I'm reminded every night as I take a trio of pills (which I swallow in the name of the Father, and in the name of the Son, and in the name of the Holy Spirit). God and medicine are keeping my leukemia from progressing. Yet, in the morning, cancer cells are reproducing again in hopes of winning the fight for my blood. Leukemia wants my body while satan wants to reign over my mind. A daily battle ensues.

In the same way, every second of every day cancer and satan prey on our bodies and minds wanting to win the big C trophy. Don't let them. Cancer may win the war for our bodies, but let's not allow satan to win the war for our minds and our souls.

And this is the secret—Christ lives in you! Who is more powerful in your life? Christ or cancer? Cancer can eat away at your bones and cells, but cancer can't touch your soul. Cancer can steal time, but cancer can't take away a moment God planned for you. Cancer will not win the victory for your life. Christ already won it. Jesus Christ is the big C. Keep your eyes on Jesus Christ the healer, not on cancer the destroyer. Cancer is vicious, but Christ is the Victory!

When our days are weary and we feel overcome by disease, singing draws us into the presence of Jesus, our healer, where we need to be every day of our journey. When life seems out of tune, sing out to Jesus!

"Christ in Me"
by A. B. Simpson

This is my wonderful story, Christ to my heart has come;
Jesus the King of Glory, finds in my heart a home.
Christ in me, Christ in me, Christ in me, O wonderful story,
Christ in me, Christ in me, Christ in me, the hope of glory.
Was there e're story so moving, story of love and pain;
Was there e're Bridegroom so loving,
seeking our heart to gain.
I am so glad I received Him, Jesus my heart's dear King;
I who so often have grieved Him, all to His feet would bring.
How can I ever be lonely, how can I ever fall;
What can I want, if only Christ is my all in all?
Now in His bosom confiding, this my glad song shall be;
I am in Jesus abiding, Jesus abides in me.
Christ in me, Christ in me, Christ in me, O wonderful story,
Christ in me, Christ in me, Christ in me, the hope of glory.

Heavenly Father, Jesus Christ, Holy Spirit, three in One, You are my hope of glory. Come live in me. Fill me. Use me. Wipe away any thought that cancer is victorious in my life. It is You, Christ, Who is my big C. May my eyes be fixed on You, Who is the giver of life — eternal life in Heaven and abundant life on earth. Keep me from the negative that brings depression, discouragement, worry, and heaviness to my heart. I shout, "Victory in the name of Jesus Christ!" God, You hold my heart. May I run my race well for Your glory and honor. Amen.

Ribbons for Your Heart

"What, then, shall we say in response to this? If God is for us, who can be against us?" (Romans 8:31 NIV). Say it out loud: "If God is for us, who can be against us?" Nothing! God is for you. Don't let the naysayers discourage you with thoughts that cancer came and God left. "Jesus said, 'All authority in heaven and earth has been given to me'" (Matthew 28:18 NIV). Not *some* authority. *All* authority! If Christ has all authority, then cancer has no authority over you. Breathe a sigh of relief and hope and thankfulness while you tie a *"Christ is my Big C"* ribbon around your heart.

Chapter 9

Dwelling in Victory

Let the word of Christ dwell in you richly as you teach and admonish one another with all wisdom, and as you sing psalms, hymns and spiritual songs with gratitude in your hearts to God (Colossians 3:16 NIV).

I love my bath. At my first writer's conference, I was advised to write about my passions. *Hmmmm.* I considered my passions and, I am embarrassed to say, the first thought that popped into my mind was, *I'm passionate about my bath.* So, now you know why my first two books were titled *Splashes of Serenity: Bathtime Reflections . . . .*

Does writing this book, *Praise the Lord and Pass the Chemo*, mean I am passionate about cancer? Yes. When we receive a cancer diagnosis, we become passionate about this disease because we have entered a battle for our lives and for the happiness of those who love us. Cancer causes even the quiet and complacent to become fierce fighters in this brutal war. Our passions are stirred.

Daily we enter the war zone. We befriend other cancer patients, trade cancer cures, read cancer blogs, search the Internet and—honestly—grow tired of talking about cancer.

We must prepare for the battle, but we don't need to dwell on the battlefield. There are greater life-enhancing weapons available to us than the latest medical breakthrough.

I love the word *dwell*. Webster defines *dwell* as "to remain for a time." I love to dwell in my bath, to remain for a time—a long time. Whatever rouses our passions, we dwell there. My husband is passionate about golf. He doesn't just hit the ball, he *dwells* on that golf course, soaking in all the green beauty and serenity. Cancer, unfortunately, dwells in us. As well, we dwell in cancer. We don't live a second of a day not thinking about the evil eating our cells. That's why cancer rouses our passions.

God tells us to "Let the word of God dwell in you . . ." (Colossians 3:16 NIV). While surgeons and medicines and healthy lifestyles thwart our cancers, the very Word of God blocks the *effects* of cancer on our physical and spiritual lives. Discouragement, fear, anger, depression, and any other darts satan throws at us in our dark days activate a cancer in our minds, which (doctors say) can stimulate cancer in our cells. Remember my oncologist's first instruction? "Get rid of all the stress in your life." Stress sets off cancer.

How do we remove the trauma of cancer in our bodies and our minds? We dwell in the Word of God. Don't just read the Bible . . . dwell there. Remain for a time, keeping our eyes and hearts focused on God's promises. "These commandments that I give you today are to be upon your hearts. Impress them on your children. Talk about them when you sit at home and when you walk along the road, when you lie down and when you get up. Tie them as symbols on your hands and bind them on your foreheads. Write them on the doorframes of your houses and on your gates" (Deuteronomy 6:6-9 NIV). Place Scripture verses on mirrors, dashboards, computers, microwaves. As we hide God's Word in our hearts, we dwell there and immerse ourselves in truth.

Years ago I loved visiting a woman I wanted to be like when I grew up. Mrs. Fisk sparkled! She always had a smile, an encouraging word, a twinkle in her eye, and a joyful spirit. Sitting by her bedside, I wanted to dwell there, for I knew I was in the presence of a holiness I desired in my life.

What made Mrs. Fisk remarkable? She knew suffering. She'd buried more than one husband and, without a mate, reared a houseful of children. Now in her nineties she stayed in bed, unable to walk—her frail frame too weak to endure the osteoporosis afflicting her bones. Diabetes had taken its toll on her sparkling eyes and left her without sight.

Blind and confined to bed, Mrs. Fisk lived victorious in her affliction because she did not look at her circumstances; she looked to her Jesus.

Beside her bed, a bulletin board displayed pictures of people she loved, including family and missionaries serving Jesus in a far-away land. Mrs. Fisk could not see those pictures, but she knew who they were and where they were on her wall and on the planet. She kept these people in her heart as she prayed for them each day.

Like many who suffer, Mrs. Fisk thought of and prayed for others more than for herself.

One day I said, "Mrs. Fisk, how do you do it? You live in pain. You can't walk or see, yet you always smile. What's the secret of your happiness? You have a peace we all want, yet so few possess?"

Without contemplating her answer, she propped herself up, raised her face close to mine, and whispered, "Why, I keep myself clean."

I laughed. There was no way she was dirty, nor did she have the capability to wash herself, so I asked, "Oh, Mrs. Fisk, how do you keep yourself clean?"

She giggled like a young girl about to tell the world her beauty secret. "I bathe in God's Word!"

There's the secret! If we want to live a victorious and joy-filled life in spite of our disease, we must bathe—immerse ourselves and dwell—in God's Word. Scripture saturated Mrs. Fisk's heart until it illuminated her eyes, flowed from her lips, and glowed on her face. Her cup was never half full—her cup ran over.

Like Mrs. Fisk, we have hard days. But when we pour the water softener of God's Word into our daily bath, life is softer and sweeter. And clean!

My mother developed cancer in her eye. She read her Bible every day, but I never knew she memorized Scripture. On the difficult day the surgeons would remove her eyeball, I searched for a Bible verse to calm her fears. Sitting with her, I began reading aloud "So do not fear, for I am with you; do not be dismayed, for I am your God . . ." (Isaiah 41:10 NIV). Before I could finish, Mother took my hand and recited the rest of the verse from her heart. "I will strengthen you and help you; I will uphold you with my righteous right hand." Years ago my mother had bathed herself in this verse, and on a day of despair and fear, the Lord brought the words of comfort and truth back to comfort her.

God tells us not only to dwell on the Word of God but also to "sing psalms, hymns and spiritual songs with gratitude in your hearts to God" (Colossians 3:16 NIV). Sing "May the Mind of Christ, My Savior" as a prayer.

"May the Mind of Christ, My Savior"
by Kate B. Wilkinson

May the mind of Christ, my Savior,
live in me from day to day,
By His love and power controlling all I do and say.
May the Word of God dwell richly
in my heart from hour to hour,
So that all may see I triumph only thru His power.
May the peace of God, my Father, rule my life in everything,
That I may be calm to comfort sick and sorrowing.
May the love of Jesus fill me, as the waters fill the sea;
Him exalting, self abasing — this is victory.
May I run the race before me,
strong and brave to face the foe,
Looking only unto Jesus as I onward go.
May His beauty rest upon me as I seek the lost to win,
And may they forget the channel, seeing only Him.

Oh, Heavenly Father, I do want my loved ones to see Jesus in me. Help me. Fill me with Your Holy Spirit. Discipline me not only to read and memorize Your Word but also to dwell in it, believe it, and live it. Clean me, Lord. Wash me with Your Word and cleanse me of any sin that makes me dirty. I want to sparkle for Jesus and live each day in victory for the glory of God. I pray in Jesus' name, amen.

Ribbons for Your Heart

"Take . . . the sword of the Spirit, which is the word of God" (Ephesians 6:17 NIV). We are in a physical and a spiritual battle. Cancer has invaded our bodies, creating casualties that mess with our minds. Let us draw our weapons—the sword of the Spirit, which is the Word of God. "For our struggle is not against [cancer], but against the . . . powers of this dark world and against the spiritual forces of evil . . ." (Ephesians 6:12 NIV, edits mine). Draw swords and wrap a *"Dwelling in Victory"* ribbon around your heart.

Chapter 10

When Cancer Hits Home

*And we know that in all things God works for the good of
those who love him . . .* (Romans 8:28 NIV).

Cancer affects every member of the family. In an instant,
life turns upside down for both the cancer patient and the
people who love them. The moment we receive a cancer
diagnosis, we realize—perhaps for the first time—how
incapable we are of protecting our families from the pain of this
disease.

Fear, anger, sorrow, despair, depression, irritability,
loneliness, and selfishness rear their ugly heads in a whirlwind
of emotions. Nobody likes it, no one would choose it, and nary
a one can change the family crisis called *cancer*.

Questions with no answers keep the family swirling in a
perpetual state of emotional turmoil. Why? Why does my son,
my sister, my mother, my loved one have cancer? Why would
God who loves us do this to us? Why me? Why my mom? Why
my baby? Why now?

First, let me assure you God did not do this to us. We live
in a fallen world where our bodies are imperfect and prone to
sickness. One day we will die, and for some death comes

sooner rather than later. God never guaranteed anyone a long and a healthy life, but He did tell us He loves us, and He will never leave us. His promises are true for cancer patients as well as for the families who love them. Nothing can separate us from the love of God. Nothing!

"Who shall separate us from the love of Christ? Shall trouble or hardship or persecution or famine or nakedness or danger or sword . . . No, in all these things we are more than conquerors through him who loved us. For I am convinced that neither death nor life, neither angels nor demons, neither the present nor the future, nor any powers, neither height nor depth, nor anything else in all creation, will be able to separate us from the love of God that is in Christ Jesus our Lord" (Romans 8:35, 37-39 NIV).

God assures us of His love no matter our troubles. Nothing can separate us. Also, He is working everything out for our good. "And we know that in all things God works for the good of those who love him, who have been called according to his purpose" (Romans 8:28 NIV).

How could this cancer, this major disruption to our lives, this awful pain, this uncertain future ever be considered good? Cancer can draw us closer to God. That's good. But cancer can cause some to doubt and question God.

When I was a teenager, God surprised my parents with a baby. Tyler was a delightful caboose in our family's train of six. Joy, laughter, and fun arrived with his birth. We all adored him. Then tragedy hit. Cancer. My bouncy, healthy, smiley baby brother had cancer. At nine months old he was given six months to live. *Why, God? Why?*

I was sixteen and I hurt. My little brother was admitted to a hospital far from home, and my parents spent their days and many nights with him. His illness and their absence hit me hard. One moment they were with me, and the next moment the three most important people in my young life were gone. My parents were where they needed to be—with my brother where he had to be—but I missed them all.

Kaboom! Cancer blew up our home like a bomb. Life as a carefree teen ended as household responsibilities fell on my unprepared shoulders. Cooking, shopping, laundering, and caring for a younger sister became my new normal. Nothing was the same. With teenage hormones raging, I experienced a mountainous mixture of emotions. Sweet dreams of teenage boys were interrupted by sobs of sorrow and sometimes screams of terror. I hurt for me. I hurt for my brother. I hurt for my parents. I hurt because I felt selfish and guilty. I just hurt.

This time was the worst of my young life. God seemed far away, and my blind eyes saw no good coming from the suffering of my fractured family.

Looking back, I realize God never lies. God was with me. God loved me. God cared. God never left. And, as promised, He worked it all out for good.

During this awful time, I learned lessons I would not have learned had my days been sweet. Our family crisis grew this self-absorbed teenager into a woman sensitive and compassionate toward others' pain. At age sixteen I realized a bad-hair day is not the end of the world, a visit to the hospital is more important than a date to the prom, and people are more precious than possessions. Above all, I learned we have a miracle-working God. My brother did not die! He continues to celebrate birthdays he was never promised.

With a smile, I affirm what so many sufferers say, "I would not have chosen this pain for my life, but I am so glad I didn't miss it."

Nancy Guthrie, in her book *Holding on to Hope*, relates her sorrowful journey. Her infant daughter, Hope, was diagnosed with a rare disease and a few months later died. Nancy wrote, ". . . God uses painful, difficult experiences of life for our ultimate good! In many cases they become the best things that ever happen to us. . . . I said to God, 'Okay, if I have to go through this, then give me everything. Teach me everything you want to teach me through this. Don't let this incredible pain be wasted in my life!'" [5]

What a beautiful prayer: *Don't let this incredible pain be wasted in my life. Teach me and my family lessons to make us better.*

The day I told my children I have cancer was the hardest experience of my life. No mother desires to hurt her child. We can't lessen the sting of bad news, but our attitudes can help heal our hurting families. When we concentrate on the positive and search for the good, we influence our loved ones to do the same.

When we focus on our sorrows, we bring ourselves down along with those who love us. Of course, we have days when we grieve, but we must not linger there. Every day focus on trusting God, believing He will not waste this awful experience causing such grief in our precious families.

Let us be aware as we experience our own grief, that all the members of our families grieve too. Everyone is grieving. Some may feel shoved into the corner and ignored as attention goes to the one who needs care. Others may lash out, misbehave, and say words they regret. Grief and the changes that cancer brings cause stress emotionally, financially, spiritually, and physically. Be quick to forgive. Hold tight to each other and make a generous effort to understand.

Pray and watch for God to work good from the hard. Take courage knowing life-lessons   learned on bumpy roads leave scars, but those scars, over time, build character. People who know suffering can become more compassionate, loving, and caring. Often they stop thinking of selfish pleasures and become sensitive to the suffering of others.

Cancer patients often say their disease drew them and their families closer to God. As He taught lessons they would not have learned in a cancer-free home, they survived and became better and stronger.

Cancer works for the good of the family, making us all aware of the preciousness of time. We wake up and realize today is the day to put our technology away and have meaningful or fun face-to-face conversations and laughs with the ones we love. Family walks and vacations we hoped to do one day now become a priority. It's all for the good.

While creating those memories, be assured we have a loving Savior who promises He will take care of our families, teach them, guide them, protect them, and mold them in ways we never could.

If there is a death, we may never heal completely from the loss, but we can ask God to make us better people because we have loved, and we know heartache. We now qualify to comfort others. Not a role any of us would choose, but one God can use.

The blind hymn-writer Fanny Crosby testified how God used the difficulties of her life and worked them for good. May we see as she did, allowing God to open our eyes to the good as He shines through our days. Remember that as our Savior led Fanny, He leads you and your family all the way.

ELAINE W. MILLER

"All the Way my Savior Leads Me"
by Fanny Crosby

All the way my Savior leads me; What have I to ask beside?

Can I doubt His tender mercy,

Who through life has been my guide?

Heav'nly peace, divinest comfort,

here by faith in Him to dwell!

For I know whate're befall me, Jesus doeth all things well.

All the way my Savior leads me,

cheers each winding path I tread,

Gives me grace for every trial,

feeds me with the living bread.

Though my weary steps may falter,

and my soul athirst may be,

Gushing from the Rock before me, Lo! A spring of joy I see.

All the way my Savior leads me;

Oh, the fullness of His grace!

Perfect rest to me is promised in my Father's blest embrace.

When my spirit, clothed immortal,

wings its flight to realms of day,

This my song through endless ages: Jesus led me all the way.

This my song through endless ages: Jesus led me all the way.

Heavenly Father, nothing will ever separate me or my family from Your love. Not illness. Not cancer. Not hair loss. Not hard nights. Not miserable days. You are here, and You do all things well. Even this, Lord, I trust that You do well. Please, Lord, care for my family when I cannot. Dry their night-time tears with Your comfort and assurance that You are with us. You didn't leave. You didn't stop loving us. Teach me and all those who surround me lessons we would not have learned otherwise. Bind satan from our lives that we would not worry, become irritable, or fearful, and then miss all You have to teach us in these days. Bind us together, Lord, as a family united for the glory of God and in Jesus' name, amen.

Ribbons for Your Heart

Does God always work for the good? Try this little exercise: fold a piece of paper in half. On the bottom half, list the painful times of your life. On the top, list your blessings. You'll be surprised how, as God works in His perfect plan, the hard experiences on the bottom move to the top of the page as blessings. Certainly, cancer would be on the bottom of our folded papers. But when we surrender to God and look for all He wants to teach us through this, cancer can creep to the top as one of the best things that happened to us and to our families. Trust Jesus and wrap a *"Trusting God's Plan"* ribbon around your heart.

Chapter 11

Cancer Wakes Up Love

For this reason a man will leave his father and mother and
be united to his wife, and the two will become one flesh
(Ephesians 5:31 NIV).

Nothing hits a couple quite as hard as a smack-in-the-heart cancer diagnosis. Perhaps for the first time in their marriage a husband and wife wake up realizing they are not two people. They are one flesh. For when one spouse has cancer, they both have cancer.

Stunned by my diagnosis, my husband and I held each other—wanting time to stop, rewind, and recalculate. Life-threatening illness was not on our dream sheet. Yet, here we were headed down a road named *Cancer* with no clue where this journey would take us or what our destination would look like.

This painful diagnosis pierced to the core of our marriage. The stab hurt but drew us closer as we united with God and each other to fight this fearsome foe. In a sacred moment, much like a renewal of our wedding vows, we each surrendered our life, our marriage, and our future to the Lordship of Jesus Christ.

"I'd do anything to trade places with you. I wish it were me and not you." My husband's perfect response touched my heart.

Dan has always affirmed his love for me. He's a flower buyer, good-morning kisser, present giver, anniversary and birthday rememberer. But until our encounter with an oncologist, he'd never vocalized that he would die for me. Dan passed the test for true love because he loved me as Jesus commanded. "Husbands, love your wives, just as Christ loved the church and gave himself up for her . . ." (Ephesians 5:25 NIV).

How blessed I am knowing the love of a man wanting to die in my place and the love of a Savior who did. Life was unraveling; yet, I never felt more tied together to my husband and my Lord.

Life-threatening illnesses jolt us awake, quiet our hearts, and cause us to appreciate the priceless gift of marriage God gives to husbands and wives. The little things about each other that once irritated become precious remembrances we treasure.

In my book, *We All Married Idiots,* I tell of my husband's idiosyncrasy which, for years, caused me to say in a too-loud voice, "Stop it!" Please understand, my husband is delightful . . . but he taps. My trumpet-playing man taps a perpetual tune, with or without his horn in hand. He taps my shoulders, the steering wheel, the dinner plate, the pulpit, and just about anything where his fingers land. One night his tapping reached a new level. Startled out of a sound sleep, I heard what I feared to be the deep-in-the-night pitter-patter of a mouse scampering across our headboard. Screaming, I soon realized there was no mouse. Dan was tapping the headboard in his sleep. His tapping annoyed me, and I was quick to tell him so.

My attitude changed some years later when Dan lay motionless in the emergency room. Not knowing if he would be alive in the morning, I held his still hands and cried out to God, "Please, let me feel his fingers tapping!" Funny, I haven't complained about that idiosyncrasy since.

Sickness forces a married couple to pause. Reality stops us in our tracks, stares us in the face, and confronts us with the sobering fact that one day one of us won't be here. The absence of a shocking diagnosis, the busyness of living, or the suddenness of accidental death can prevent couples from experiencing this pause, robbing them of precious days and last moments together.

Let us hold dear this time so we may say as a friend told me, "The last six months that my husband fought his battle with cancer were probably the most precious times of our marriage."

Time. Yes, even time to discuss our death. The funeral, the burial, our last wishes. These conversations may not seem like a blessing, but what a gift it is to our loved ones when we make our preferences known now instead of forcing our families to deal with these decisions in the fury of grief. *Five Wishes* is an excellent legal resource (available in thirty-six states) which walks us through end-of-life-issues. Most doctors have copies in their offices. Information is available on their website, www.agingwithdignity.org.

Cancer can wake up love, but not always. One husband complained that he was tired of it all. His wife's cancer was robbing him of the fun he expected in marriage. Another spouse couldn't (or wouldn't) deal with the many challenges of cancer. Unable to cope, he left his beloved to go it alone.

For those in difficult marriages or no marriage at all, my heart aches for you. I find few words that will make you feel better. Please consider this unchanging truth: there is a God who loves you and who will never leave you. He promises to be your comforter and hold you close to His heart. He promises to be a husband to the husbandless. Certainly, an absentee spouse is not what you planned or expected on your wedding day. Cancer should not end your marriage, but for some it does. If this is your reality, hold tight to the best husband of all, Jesus Christ—who loves you so much that He died for you.

Healthy couples may live their whole married life without any thought that today, this month, or this year might be their last. In a cancer-marriage, a husband and wife live moment to moment with that reality. Because of that enlightenment, we treasure each other, do nice things, show respect, bring flowers, appreciate life, and love in ways we may have missed otherwise.

If your spouse has cancer, now is the time to assure your sweetheart you will never leave—you'll be there through it all. Realize you both hurt as one flesh. For the cancer patient destructive emotions abound without warning and nip at our self-esteem. We can feel ugly, scarred, inadequate . . . that we're a disappointment and a burden to our spouse. Please assure your loved one that wherever this road takes you, you are on it together—as one flesh—all the way.

Cancer may take away the length of our days, but cancer can also add breadth to our days as we open the gift of time.

Time to:

- Do now all you wanted to do together, but never made the time.
- Take that second (or third, or fourth, or . . .) honeymoon or family vacation.
- Show your children how "for better or for worse, in sickness and in health" is lived out.
- Share wisdom with your children and grandchildren.
- Forgive and ask forgiveness.
- Kiss.
- Hold hands.
- Take walks.
- Make love.
- Say "I love you."
- Be a better spouse.
- Cherish.
- Love.
- Touch.
- Stop arguing.
- Be kind.
- Look into each other's eyes when you speak or when you are quiet.
- Listen.
- Smile.
- Laugh.
- Be thankful.
- Love deeply.

- Say good bye.
- Say words that need to be said.

Do you remember the songs sung on your wedding day? Now is the time to sing them again. Relive the hope and joy and promises made the day you two became one flesh in sickness and in health. *Joyful, Joyful We Adore Thee* played as we floated down our wedding aisle, joyfully adoring each other and our God. We meant the words then and we mean them even more now.

"Joyful, Joyful, We Adore Thee"
by Henry van Dyke Jr.

Joyful, joyful, we adore Thee, God of glory, Lord of love;

Hearts unfold like flow'rs before Thee,

opening to the sun above.

Melt the clouds of sin and sadness;

drive the dark of doubt away.

Giver of immortal gladness, fill us with the light of day!

All Thy words with joy surround Thee,

earth and heav'n reflect Thy rays.

Stars and angels sing around Thee,

center of unbroken praise.

Field and forest, vale and mountain,

flowery meadow, flashing sea,

Chanting bird and flowing fountain call us to rejoice in Thee!

Thou art giving and forgiving, ever blessing, ever blest,

Well spring of the joy of living, ocean depth of happy rest!

Thou our Father, Christ our Brother —

all who live in love are Thine.

Teach us how to love each other, lift us to the joy divine!

Mortals, join the mighty chorus

which the morning stars began;

Love divine is reigning o'er us,

leading us with mercy's hand.

Ever singing, march we onward,

victors in the midst of strife.

Joyful music leads us sunward in the triumph song of life!

Heavenly Father, thank You for my marriage. In the trials and pain and stress of this disease, I pray You bind us together and keep us as one flesh in the name of the Father and of the Son and of the Holy Spirit. Prevent satan from attacking our marriage. The devil wants us to fail, but You desire we grow stronger. Fill us with Your Holy Spirit and give us love, joy, peace, patience, kindness, self control, gentleness, and goodness toward each other. These days are hard, and beautiful, and precious. Use the time to strengthen our bond as we cling to You and to each other. Make us better together, Lord Jesus, as we trust in You. Amen.

Ribbons for Your Heart

A man asked my husband, "How is your wife's cancer affecting your marriage?" He answered, "I'm learning to be a better husband." What a sweetie! Decide each day to be a better spouse, so there will be no regrets. Let your children see the sacrificial, all-encompassing, willing-to-die-in-your-place love of Jesus. Tie a *"Cancer Makes My Marriage Better"* ribbon around your heart and go kiss your honey!

Chapter 12

Break Out of the Cancer Prison

About midnight Paul and Silas were praying and singing hymns to God, and the other prisoners were listening to them (Acts 16:25 NIV).

Cancer can make us feel like a prisoner in our own bodies. From our hearts we shout, *Cut it out! Chemo it out! Radiate it out! Just get it out! Please release me from this cancer prison! I don't deserve this! I did nothing wrong!*

The Apostle Paul knew what it was like to be in prison. He was attacked, stripped, beaten, and severely flogged. His feet shackled in the stocks, he was put into the inner cell. Sort of sounds like us when cancer attacks, strips, beats, flogs, and throws us into prison. We feel fastened in stocks, hurting, hopeless, and powerless to release ourselves from this involuntary confinement. Cancer grabs hold and refuses to let go.

We never chose cancer prison. Our good behavior won't get us out early. But, we can choose how we live this incarceration. Will we fall into the depths of despair, self-pity, anger, and bitterness? Or will we count our blessings and praise the Lord?

Paul makes me smile. I want his attitude. Prison didn't crush him or cause him to fall or falter in his assurance that God was in control. By faith Paul knew God had a plan and a purpose for him in that prison. We read this account of Paul's first night behind bars: "About midnight Paul and Silas were praying and singing hymns to God, and the other prisoners were listening to them" (Acts 16:25 NIV). Good for Paul! He sang hymns and other prisoners listened to him. I suspect each prisoner's mood was lifted that night listening to Paul.

A song can transform the atmosphere of a home or a hospital or a prison from dreadful to delightful. Sweet music ministers to our own hearts as well as the hearts of fellow prisoners, those caring for us, and those loving us.

My friend Mrs. Harris had a beautiful voice, although I never heard her sing. Over forty years she lived in her own prison. Surgery after surgery cut her face away inch by inch. The lower half of her jaw and her nose nearly gone, she hid her face with a handkerchief. But scars and scarves never covered her sparkling, Jesus-shining eyes.

The need for yet another surgery hit her hard and hurt deep. This time her tongue would be cut out. Never again would she speak or sing.

"You know what makes me saddest?" she shared before her surgery. "I'll never again be able to tell my husband, 'I love you.'"

Think about it. Suppose your tongue is being cut out. For some, those thoughts may be your cancer reality. What are the last words you would say knowing you would never speak again? I joke that on my tombstone I want the words, "Toodle-oo!" So, I envision myself making light of the heaviness and rolling into the operating room with a hearty, "Toodle-oo!" Others may feel the severity of the moment, and different sentences come to mind. *I love you. Thank you. Don't leave me. Why is this awful happening to me? I hate cancer. I'm sorry. Forgive me. Hold me. Where are you, God? Jesus loves me. I'm trusting God. Pray for me. Take care of the children. Help me, God.*

Dan and I joined Mrs. Harris and her husband in the recovery room to pray. Her head imprisoned in bandages, only her eyes were visible. Oh, how, even under sedation, those eyes twinkled with peace and joy and Jesus.

"You want to know the last words she said before they cut out her tongue?" her husband said smiling.

"Oh, for a thousand tongues to sing my great Redeemer's praise!" were her last spoken words. Wow!

In Mrs. Harris we see a modern-day Paul singing in her prison for all the world to hear and read about for generations to come. Generations that will listen and watch to see what Jesus is like. When they listen to us, what will they hear and see? When the prison shuts you in, don't think about the locks and bars and restrictions. Instead, praise the Lord and sing!

"Oh, for a Thousand Tongues to Sing"
by Charles Wesley

Oh, for a thousand tongues to sing
my great Redeemer's praise,
The glories of my God and King, the triumphs of His grace.
Jesus! the name that charms our fears,
that bids our sorrow cease;
'Tis music in the sinner's ears, 'tis life and health and peace.
He breaks the power of canceled sin,
He sets the prisoner free;
His blood can make the foulest clean,
His blood availed for me.
Glory to God, and praise and love be ever, ever given
By saints below and saints above,
the Church in earth and heaven.

Heavenly Father, thank You for gifting us with music. What peace comes from singing songs of praise to You. In my lightest day and in my darkest night, may I sing for You. May my prayers and songs be a sweet, sweet sound in Your ear as the words and sounds minister to my heart and to those who are listening. In Jesus' name, amen.

Ribbons for Your Heart

Fill your home with singing! Stack your I-Pod deck with songs that praise our God and bless your spirit. Beware of satan's attempts to mute the music. Don't let him. Be like Paul. Pray and sing hymns of praise. Music brings peace to you as well as to others who are listening. Create memories by singing songs by yourself and with your family. Remember Paul and Mrs. Harris and sing, for singing truly does open prison doors and set the captives free. Shout to the Lord and tie an *"I Sing Praises to the Lord"* ribbon around your heart.

Chapter 13

God's Radiation Therapy

I sought the Lord, and he answered me; he delivered me from all my fears. Those who look to him are radiant; their faces are never covered with shame (Psalm 34:4-5 NIV).

Cancer changes everything. Our world turns upside down, hopes vanish, and dreams never come true. Hospitalization, radiation, and chemotherapy keep us from completing goals we set when we believed the glory days would never end. Cancer makes no one's bucket or "to-do" list. Yet, here we are living days consumed with treatments we pray will place us on the survivors' list.

Pain and suffering are universal. Even those without cancer have down days. Some live life one tragedy after another. Our life's race may make abrupt turns from the routes we envisioned and planned for our futures. God has a road for each of us to travel. The road can be steep and hard — a path we would never choose. Easy Street is more appealing, less harsh, and more fun, but not always in God's providence.

Bessie Miller knew about disappointments and shattered plans. Even so, she was a delight. With a glow and a joy on her face, she radiated Christ.

Bessie had a call on her life and a vision in her heart to serve Jesus on foreign soil. God's will was her passion, and she graduated from the Missionary Training Institute excited and prepared to embark on the career God ordained for her. Being in God's will and obedient to His call was Bessie's focus.

Before ever touching the ground of a foreign field, Bessie became ill. Her future began to unravel. Confined to bed for months at a time, she could not dispute the mission board's decision to change the course of her life. For her own good and because of her failing health, she would remain in the United States. Did Bessie's world fall apart? Yes and no.

Bessie never married, never had children, never left this country. None of her girlhood dreams came true. Instead, submitted and surrendered to the will of God, she joyfully served Jesus in a small church, impacting many lives in the congregation and in the community. Impacting me.

Bessie and I met when she was well into her tenth decade. As a young woman, she was too sick to serve overseas, yet in her nineties she was strong and vibrant, full of energy and love for her Jesus, His church, and lost people. Bessie could have spent her life as a victim of the Missions Board—bitter and angry with God and humans who changed the course of her life. Instead, she chose to trust Jesus and not let satan win the battle to destroy her and distract her from her goal of glorifying God.

In one word, I would describe Bessie as *radiant*! Even in her old age she radiated Christ with her sweet smile, her bright eyes, her calm spirit, her loving heart, her tender ways, and her love for all people. So, I was not surprised by her answer when I asked, "What is your favorite Bible verse?"

Without hesitation, she replied, "Oh, Psalm 34. I love Psalm 34!"

Indeed, Bessie lived Psalm 34.

"I will extol the Lord at all times; his praise will always be on my lips. My soul will boast in the Lord; let the afflicted hear and rejoice. Glorify the Lord with me; let us exalt his name together. I sought the Lord, and he answered me; he delivered me from all my fears. Those who look to him are radiant; their faces are never covered with shame" (Psalm 34:1-5 NIV).

True to Psalm 34:5, Bessie looked to Jesus, her face radiated Christ, and she was never put to shame. No matter what her day held, whether sickness or health, she looked to Jesus and reflected her King. Bessie's focus never blurred. Her faith never wavered. Her example taught me to do the same.

"Bessie just glows," I remember saying to a friend.

We laugh and refer to radiation therapy as "making us glow." I'm told we don't literally glow, but the joke is good for levity when we're about to be "fried alive." Just kidding! My friend tells me radiation therapy can be painful and uncomfortable. Killing cancer cells and shrinking tumors bring out the big guns. We muster all our grit and courage, ascend the radiation table, submit to being taped down, masked, and molded as we wait to be incinerated. (I'm trying to make jokes. Probably not a joking matter, but you get it, don't you?)

How can we get through these treatments and keep radiating Christ? By looking to Jesus. By praying, singing hymns, quoting Scriptures, and picturing our loved ones who make all this pain worth it. A friend dreaded the radiation treatments until she decided to use the time to talk to her Jesus. She prayed not only for herself but also for all her family, friends, and fellow cancer patients. The curse of radiation became a blessing as she drew near to God. Also, radiation works! It destroys cancer cells and shrinks tumors—and a cancer patient lives! Hallelujah!

Moses was another whose face was radiant. "When Moses came down from Mount Sinai with the two tablets of the Testimony in his hands, he was not aware that his face was radiant because he had spoken with the Lord" (Exodus 34:29 NIV). Moses spoke to the Lord and his face was radiant.

While lying on our radiation, chemotherapy, or operating tables, we can radiate fear, dread, anxiety, and anger. Or, we can radiate Christ. Where our thoughts dwell, there we will stay. With our eyes on Jesus and our hearts praying to Him, we fight our biggest foe—the devil's battle for our minds. Don't let satan win! After all, he already lost. Jesus won this victory, and He holds us in His hands!

Sandi Banks writes in *Anchors of Hope*, "Pain 101—the class no one signs up for but everyone benefits from—is usually the source of the greatest education of our lifetimes. We learn who God is, who we are, and who He and we can be together."[6] Isn't that a class we all want to sign up for?

Pain is a great teacher. We learn valuable lessons when we give God our undivided attention. Look up. Pay attention. Don't miss what God has for us in this battle.

Albert Schweitzer wrote, "Where did you catch a glimpse of the higher Destiny of your life? In suffering. Where did you feel God was near to you? In suffering. Where did you first realize the blessedness of having a Father in Heaven? In suffering."[7]

As radiation kills our cancer cells and shrinks our tumors, God's radiation therapy kills our fears, calms our anxieties, and revives our spirits. Jump up on the Heavenly Father's therapy table, be ready to fight, and be armed for the battle. Look to God. Speak to Him. Radiate Him. Now, that's a therapy we will enjoy!

When we sing happy tunes while driving to the cancer centers and while enduring our treatments, we'll radiate Jesus, and Son-shine will fill our souls.

"Sunshine in my Soul"
by Eliza E. Hewitt

There is sunshine in my soul today,
more glorious and bright
Than glows in any earthly sky, for Jesus is my light.
There is music in my soul today, a carol to my King;
And Jesus listening, can hear the songs I cannot sing.
There is springtime in my soul today,
for when the Lord is near,
The dove of peace sings in my heart,
the flowers of grace appear.
There is gladness in my soul today,
and hope and praise and love.
For blessings which He gives me now,
for joys laid up above.
Oh, there's sunshine, blessed sunshine,
While the peaceful, happy moments roll;
When Jesus shows His smiling face,
there is sunshine in my soul.

Heavenly Father, thank You for radiation therapy — medical radiation that kills my cancer and spiritual radiation that kills my fears. Radiating Christ is my goal. I do want to shine for You so people see Jesus in me. Help me, Lord. When I am being infused, chemoed, radiated, cut open, cut out, or cut off, may I look to You and speak to You and radiate You. Heal my broken spirit, Lord, as well as my diseased body. You are the Son-shine of my soul. Thank You for holding me and keeping me warm on those rainy days when the Son seems to disappear. I know You don't leave. You promise, and You never lie. May I shine for You in Jesus' name, amen.

Ribbons for Your Heart

On a stormy Seattle morning, Dan and I were flying home to Syracuse. The sky was black. Not a peak of sunshine. *Surely our flight will be cancelled,* I thought. Faint with fear I boarded the airplane, sure someone would have the sense to delay take-off until the storm subsided. As we lifted into the blackness, the most glorious sight appeared out my window. Within seconds of our ascent, my eyes were blinded by the brightness of the sun. I had to turn away, but not before seeing the blackness below and the brilliance above. Cancer and our treatments for this disease may seem like dark places, but directly over the gloom is our most magnificent God shining His light on us. When we focus on Him and speak to Him, His radiance touches our hearts and we radiate, too. What a picture of God's omnipresence! With confidence, tie an *"I am Radiant"* ribbon around your heart.

Chapter 14

The Blessings of Cancer

. . . the Lord your God . . . turned the curse into a blessing
for you, because the Lord your God loves you
(Deuteronomy 23:5 NIV).

Is cancer a curse or a blessing? Easy answer. Of course, cancer is a curse as defined by Webster, "an evil or misfortune that has been invoked upon one." Yet, for many who wear the cancer ribbons, this dreaded disease is a blessing. In fact, some say cancer is the best thing that ever happened to them.

Webster defines a blessing as, "something that . . . does good for a person."[8] Some Bible scholars say a blessing is "anything that brings you closer to God." The Hebrew word for "blessing" is "esher" which means "happiness." Will cancer be good for us? Could this curse bring us to God or closer to Him? For sure, *cancer* and *happiness* are not synonyms. Or are they?

God says because He loves us, he will turn this curse into a blessing. Let's see how God works out the promise of Deuteronomy 23:5 in the lives of those living with the cancer curse.

I noticed cancer patients were different the moment I stepped into a cancer center waiting room. There was a heavenly peace, calm, patience, and joy rarely found in the streets of our towns or the aisles of our grocery stores. This truth hit me when a frazzled shopper raged at another shopper as their carts collided. My first thought was, *I can't wait to go to the cancer center where people are nice to each other.* There, people live life less in the world and more in the eternal.

There are many ways cancer is a blessing. Here are a few:

Cancer is a blessing because the ugly of the world grows dim and the beauty of Heaven shines bright as cancer carries us deep into the heart of Jesus. This disease strips us of earthly dependence and throws us naked into the arms of God. What a great place to land! There is no fig leaf of self-confidence to hide our utter need of God when cancer crumbles our worldly facade.

Cancer is a blessing because sickness causes us to set our minds and our hearts on things above, not on earthly things. The things of this world can discourage, distract, and deflate. Daily fixing our thoughts on Heaven, God's power, His providence, and His sovereignty is a blessing we can miss when we are healthy.

When we focus on God, we experience His peace, comfort, strength, joy, and love. If we choose to fight this disease with human strength, we arm ourselves with the weakness of the world. Our minds fill with fear, anger, worry . . . every negative concoction the devil stirs up to sap our depleted energy.

Cancer is a blessing because a terminal illness shortens life but lengthens days as our eyes open to the beauty we often miss in our every-day blind busyness. When death looks us in the eye, we realize what is significant in life as we shut out the trivial.

Cancer is a blessing because sickness changes us and makes us better. Through suffering God teaches us life-lessons we never would have learned otherwise, and we are thankful we didn't miss.

Many afflicted with cancer attest that God turned their curse into a blessing. I asked a few of my cancer friends if they thought cancer was a blessing. Here are their thoughts and mine:

"Cancer . . . sharpens my resolve to add positively to the day for everyone I encounter," Rick shared from his hospice bed. His curse had become a blessing in his life as well as the lives of those who visited him at home or online.

I must add a hearty, "Me, too!" Shortly after my diagnosis, my heart changed. Making every day count for me personally, as well as for those God put in my path, became a daily resolve. I decided I would smile and be kind to every person I met. Being grumpy was no longer an option. Cancer made me realize every grouchy day is a day not lived. Time is too short and people are too precious. Offering kindness and a smile, extending a helping hand, and sharing a sweet hello blessed others and made me happy. Why does it take cancer for us to discover the joy we give others comes back multiplied?

Cancer is good for us because our eyes open to what is important in life. We determine to set better priorities. Joe flew to Colorado with his son and to Georgia with his daughter. He said, "I would not have done those things without the cancer. I would have been too occupied with work."

I also determined to make time with my family a higher priority. Dan and I went on a sibling tour to Tennessee, North Carolina, and Pennsylvania. If laughter cures cancer, then I'm healed! What memories we created. Cancer nudges us to create memories we may have missed thinking we still had time. No one has assurance of tomorrow. Death for the sick and the healthy can come suddenly. Cancer alerts us to this reality and alters our priorities and plans.

Charlene, the mother of a cancer patient, shared, "A cancer diagnosis teaches a completely new way to trust Jesus day by day . . . moment by moment."

True. Cancer called me to complete trust and surrender to God's will. Realizing my inability to be in command of what happens in my body (or my child's body), I gave up control and handed the reins to Jesus. What freedom we experience and stress we relinquish when we stop striving and trust ourselves and our families to the Almighty God.

"Never before have I experienced the all-encompassing peace of God as I did through the cancer experience. I was wrapped in His peace," Rhonda said.

We can't explain this, but, as He promised, when we need Him most, Jesus shows up and wraps us in His love. Never have I known His peace and calm and trust like the day cancer arrived. As though Jesus knew all the time this cancer would happen (and He did know, by the way), He seemed to be waiting in the wings of my life for the glorious day I would embrace Him as He held me.

Cancer is a blessing to marriage. Marriage celebrations go from ho-hum to hallelujah! When we know each day could be our last, we treasure our spouses in ways we took for granted before diagnosis.

Cancer is a blessing when we experience the Holy Spirit's peace. Debbi said, "I read about that peace that passes understanding, had prayed for it for myself and others, but through my cancer journey, I got to live that peace."

Pretty mysterious how God knows exactly what we need and when we need that Holy Spirit peace. Many realize this peace in their hearts in ways they never experienced before cancer. In my mind I pictured myself frantic, distraught, and devastated at the thought of being told I have leukemia. Instead, as the oncologist gave me the news, I felt calm, composed, and at peace. Three years later, still with cancer, I continue to know peace that passes all understanding.

Cancer is a blessing when God brings new people into our lives to pray for and to love. Debbi tells us, "One of the things God has given me is a stronger desire to pray for others who are struggling with cancer. I have a dry-erase board on my refrigerator filled with names of folks walking the cancer walk, and it is my joy to pray for each soul represented on that board. I would never have known about these folks were it not for my own cancer diagnosis. I thank God He has used it mightily."

Cancer is a blessing when God gives us time to grow closer to Him, to say good-bye to our families, and to appreciate small joys like walks in the garden. Mary said, "A friend had renewed energy and was able to work in his yard and grow his garden. His faith in God grew, and the Lord blessed him with time with his wife and family to say good-bye."

Cancer is a blessing when prayer for ourselves and with our families becomes a greater priority. Mary wrote, "God delivered a friend from a disease that was ravaging his body. He and his wife spent hours in prayer." Hours in prayer together! I suspect those hours were the dearest hours of their marriage. What a blessing!

Cancer is a blessing when we receive fresh courage and faith. Mary concluded, "God filled him with such faith and courage as the disease progressed, an extreme blessing. And Jesus ushered him safely home into His arms that day he left our presence, the ultimate blessing as we pass from this life into eternity."

Cancer is a blessing because I became less interested in the daily news, which changes every day, and, instead, focus on the unchanging word of God and His promises to me. God knows what we need, and the Bible is filled with encouragement for each day. Promises like, ". . . this is what the Lord says—he who created you . . . 'Fear not, for I have redeemed you; I have called you by name; you are mine. When you pass through the waters, I will be with you; and when you pass through the rivers, they will not sweep over you. When you walk through the fire, you will not be burned, the flames will not set you ablaze. For I am the Lord, your God, the Holy One of Israel, your Savior . . . Since you are precious and honored in my sight, and because I love you . . . Do not be afraid, for I am with you'" (Isaiah 43:1-5 NIV).

Cancer is a blessing because I now rub shoulders with the courageous and strong. Cancer sufferers are like family because they share a life-experience others do not. My trips to cancer centers bought me more than I could purchase at the shopping centers because my brothers and sisters with cancer showed me how to live life better. I am blessed watching them:

- Smile and greet everyone.
- Make each moment a God-moment.
- Purposefully bless people wherever they go.
- Live in the reality that this day could be their last, so they live joyful, live full, and live well.
- Look for opportunities to talk to and pray with other patients.
- Give because they know there is no reason to keep.
- Purpose to bestow a kind word of encouragement to every human they see.
- Give back all the kindness people give to them.
- Live each day to the full.

Venita McCart, author of *It's Cancer — Finding Help and Hope on the Road to Recovery*, has been through lung cancer twice since 2000. Venita shared with me that, "The eternal perspective gained, the trust He builds, and the intimacy with the Lord Jesus that He graces are   light years beyond our human understanding. And He teaches us hope, peace, and strength at an eternal level beyond mere human belief."

Cancer is a blessing because God gives us heavenly perspective. My friend Kathy sums up the whole of cancer as a blessing:

"Throughout this experience, my eyes began to shift from the ground up to Heaven. I began to see the hand of God in this hardship when before I couldn't see beyond my own nose. I began to know my Savior as I had never known Him before. I felt His love so powerful that it overshadowed the suffering. He was so close that I began to feel how His heart feels and not my own. I would open my eyes, and He was right there with me. He never left my side. I was never alone.

"If I could change that diagnosis, I wouldn't, for what I now know about my Lord through it. You see when a person nears the door of eternity, the view changes — at least mine did. I took off the rose-colored glasses of the world and put on the true colors of eternal eyes."[9]

Cancer is a curse if we focus on the devastation happening in our bodies. Depression, grief, sadness, and anger are normal reactions. Don't deny the curse of cancer, but don't let the curse destroy you. God says he will turn the curse into a blessing. Trust Him.

Cancer is a blessing when we set our minds on God and His promises. Realize the victory and receive the blessing when we fix our hearts, our eyes, and our minds on the eternal, not on the earthly.

A.B. Simpson knew adversity, affliction, and illness. The following hymn compares life lived in the world versus life lived in the Lord. When we surrender our disease to the Lordship of Christ, then we will experience the blessings of cancer.

"Himself"

by Albert B. Simpson

Once it was the blessing, now it is the Lord;
Once it was the feeling, now it is His Word;
Once His gift I wanted, now the Giver own;
Once I sought the healing, now Himself alone . . .
All in all forever, only Christ I'll sing;
Everything in Jesus, and Jesus everything.
Once 'twas painful trying, now 'tis perfect trust;
Once a half salvation, now the uttermost,
Once 'twas ceaseless holding, now He holds me fast;
Once 'twas constant drifting, now my anchor's cast.
Once 'twas busy planning, now 'tis trustful prayer;
Once 'twas anxious caring, now He has the care;
Once 'twas what I wanted, now what Jesus says;
Once 'twas constant asking, now tis ceaseless praise.
Once it was my working, His it hence shall be;
Once I tried to use Him, now He uses me;
Once the pow'r I wanted, now the Mighty One;
Once for self I labored, now for Him alone.
Once I hoped in Jesus, now I know He's mine;
Once my lamps were dying, now they brightly shine;
Once for death I waited, now His coming Hail;
And my hopes are anchored safe within the veil.
All in all forever, only Christ I sing;
Everything in Jesus, and Jesus everything.

Heavenly Father, Your Word says to thank You for everything. Jesus, You are my everything. Thank You for opening my eyes to truth and beauty and love. I missed much before this cancer, but You gave me clearer eyes, a holier mind, and a new life when You allowed me to have this affliction. So, I thank You for cancer. Thank You for lessons You are teaching me. Thank You for loving me, for never leaving me, for caring for me. In the dark You hold me close, and You promise to never let me go. May I not focus on the pain but on the promise of Your constant care. Keep my eyes and mind fixed on eternity and not on the worries of this world. You've got this, Lord, and You've got me in the palm of Your hand. Thank You for never letting go. In Jesus' name, amen.

Ribbons for Your Heart

From his hospice bed, my friend Rick said, "Every moment is a miracle waiting for us to notice." Don't miss your moments or your miracles. Life is a gift and each day a blessing to celebrate. Celebrate now! Every morning is a wake-up call to live this day to the full. Treasure each breath as sacred. Let cancer make you better and draw you closer to God as you fix your heart, your eyes, and your mind on the eternal and not the earthly. Cancer is a curse that God turns into a blessing because He loves you. Rejoice and thank God as you tie a *"Cancer is a Blessing"* ribbon around your heart.

Chapter 15

Why Are We so Afraid of Heaven?

*He will wipe every tear from their eyes. There will be no
more death or mourning or crying or pain, for the old order
of things has passed away* (Revelation 21:4 NIV).

The doctor didn't look me in the eye (not a good sign). "Your medicine could stop working at any time. You could die in three weeks. We need a Plan B. You should consider a bone marrow transplant."

The next doctor looked me straight in the eye (not necessarily a good sign, either). "Do you realize a transplant could kill you in three weeks?"

A second, third, or fourth opinion is essential when our treatment path is not clear. Please don't trust the brain of only one physician. I've learned oncologists don't all think alike.

Cancer is like a roller coaster. We never know from one appointment to the next whether we will be at the top or making a fast descent to the pits of this disease. One month celebrating, the next month mourning. I've never been a fan of roller coasters.

To transplant or not to transplant—that was the question. I spent the next months consumed with gathering information from more oncologists, transplant teams, out-of-state cancer centers, books, Internet, friends, and especially the Lord Jesus. Caution: when searching the Internet, believe only reliable, recommended, and recent posts. Cancer research makes daily breakthroughs. Accurate information three months ago may be outdated today.

"Flip a coin," said one doctor. "Roll the dice," said another. Doctors don't know everything, but God does, and He isn't flipping coins or rolling dice. Hallelujah! In my mind the question was simply, *would I rather die from cancer or from a bone marrow transplant?* Either answer seemed to point to one destination—Heaven.

Peace was my companion on this journey, knowing whatever road I travelled I'd be on God's road for me. God could heal me via a transplant or He could keep my medicine working. Best yet, God could outright heal me. I asked Jesus to make this decision easy. We do not have a God of confusion. So, I prayed (and asked many friends to pray) that I would be certain, not confused, and that His will for me would be clear.

And clear it was! The Federal Drug Administration approved a new drug, and it's now available to replace my current chemo when it stops working. The bone marrow transplant and thoughts of *I may die in three weeks* were off the table. Up, up, up climbed my roller coaster once again.

Today, I rejoice and thank God my medicines are working, and my blood counts are normal. As I settle into my life's routine with no thoughts of dying in three weeks, or in three years, I realize God has again taught me lessons on this journey and caused me to ask the question:

Why are we so afraid to go to Heaven?

We plead with God to heal us and not take us there. We want to stay here. Why? Human instinct, I suppose. Personally, I look forward to Heaven, but the process of getting there frightens me. Pain is not my forte.

I'm not in love with the things of this earth. Yet, I don't want to die. Heaven sounds wonderful, but thoughts of missing Christmases, family weddings, great grandchildren, and much more keep me yearning to stay here. I know this earth doesn't need me to keep it turning. Life goes on. Our families grieve and then laugh again. But still . . .

Today God has granted us life, but one day will be our final day. God is teaching me to live and die well. Like Paul, I say, "For to me, to live is Christ and to die is gain" (Philippians 1:21 NIV).

We fear death, but God tells us not to fear. He is with us. Always. The days we live and the day we die.

I held my father's hand as he took his final breath. I sensed the very hand of God touching mine as He slipped my dad's hand into His and escorted my daddy Home. A believer's death is sacred. Glorious. Holy. "Precious in the sight of the Lord is the death of his saints" (Psalm 116:15 NIV). What is precious to God should never fill us with fear, but with acceptance and trust in the One who holds us and will never let go.

Death—that dreaded day—promises to be the greatest moment of our lives. When we see our Lord Jesus face to face, as we enter the Holy City, God Himself wipes every tear from our eyes, and all pain is gone: no chemo, no infusions, no blood tests, no radiation, no sickness, no mourning, no death. The blind see, the lame walk, our old bodies become new. Oh, imagine the celestial colors, the sights, and the sounds of Heaven! The singing! No more bad news. Ever. No sin. No shame. No satan.

God tells us to ". . . set your hearts on things above, where Christ is seated at the right hand of God. Set your minds on things above, not on earthly things" (Colossians 3:1-2 NIV). To live and die victoriously, we must live in the heavenlies on this earth, with our eyes, our hearts, and our minds set on things above, not on earthly things. The world will pass away. We will pass from this world. But God has prepared a permanent place for us. How wonderful eternal life with Him will be. No more death. No more roller coasters. I am not afraid. I'm excited to go there, aren't you?

"My Jesus, I Love Thee"
by William R. Featherstone

My Jesus, I love Thee, I know Thou art mine.
For Thee all the follies of sin I resign;
My gracious Redeemer, my Saviour art Thou,
If ever I loved Thee, my Jesus, 'tis now.
I love Thee because Thou has first loved me,
And purchased my pardon on Calvary's tree;
I love Thee for wearing the thorns on Thy brow;
If ever I loved Thee, my Jesus, 'tis now.
I'll love Thee in life, I will love Thee in death,
And praise Thee as long as Thou lendest me breath;
And say, when the death dew lies cold on my brow,
If ever I loved Thee, my Jesus, 'tis now.
In mansions of glory and endless delight,
I'll ever adore Thee in heaven so bright;
I'll sing with the glittering crown on my brow,
If ever I loved Thee, my Jesus, 'tis now.

Heavenly Father, thank You for preparing a place for us in Heaven. May I keep my eyes and my mind and my heart on the eternal and not on the earthly. I do pray You will comfort my family. I hurt when they hurt, and I know while I go to the peaceful place, they stay in the turmoil. Strengthen them, Lord. Help them keep their eyes on Jesus and follow You all the days of their lives until that soon and glorious day we meet again on the Heavenly shores.

Ribbons for Your Heart

Dear friends, may we all believe like Paul, who said, "For to me, to live is Christ and to die is gain" (Philippians 1:21 NIV). Live! Live today looking forward to and not fearing Heaven. Run your race every day in victory until that glorious day we cross the finish line, rip off all our ribbons and shout, **"Praise the Lord! There's no more cancer!"**

ENDNOTES

[1] https://www.cancercenter.com/treatments/laughter-therapy/.

[2] http://www.eaec.org/faithhallfame/fanny_ crosby.htm.

[3] Hannah Whitall Smith, *The Christian's Secret of a Happy Life* (New York; Ballantine Books, 1942, repr. 1970), 190.

[4] https://www.merriam-webster.com/dictionary/angel

[5] Nancy Guthrie, *Holding On to Hope* (Carol Stream, IL: Tyndale House, 2002), 44.

[6] Sandi Banks, *Anchors of Hope* (Nashville: Broadman&Holman Publishers, 2002), 75.

[7] http://www.angelfire.com/journal/pacrome/schweitzerpage.html.

[8] https://www.merriam-webster.com/thesaurus/blessing

[9] Kathy Murtha, *Tell Me a Story*, Fulton Alliance Church, (Fulton, NY, 2015), 129-130.

Made in the USA
Columbia, SC
05 May 2020